A Memoir of the Miracles and Wonder of God

Jesus Shattered my Religion

Suzanne Kutz

Jesus Shattered My Religion

Published by Suzanne Kutz | Huntingdon, Pennsylvania

ISBN (Print): 979-8-9854849-0-8

ISBN (Kindle): 979-8-9854849-1-5

Library of Congress Control Number (LCCN): 2021925335

Printed in the United States of America

Prepared for Publication: www.wendykwalters.com

To contact the author: suzanne-kutz.com

Scripture Translations Used

Dedication

This book is dedicated to
my Lord and Savior, Jesus Christ,
all those who have yet to meet Him,
to my two beautiful daughters, Kelly and Kimberly,
and the generations to come.
With special acknowledgment to the Holy Spirit, who
inspired and scribed much of this book.

In sorrowful memory of
Steven K. Kutz
1955-2010

Medical Disclaimer

The author is not a medical professional and recognizes that there are people who need to seek medical and psychiatric help apart from spiritual issues. The contents of *Jesus Shattered My Religion* is not intended to substitute for professional medical advice, diagnosis, or treatment. Always seek the advice of your physician or another qualified health provider with any questions you may have regarding a medical condition. Never disregard professional medical advice or delay in seeking it because of something you have read in this book. If you think you may have a medical emergency, call your doctor, go to the emergency room, or call 911 immediately.

Praise for
Jesus Shattered My Religion

It is my privilege to recommend this amazing and powerful book, *Jesus Shattered My Religion,* by Sue Kutz. Sue is a graduate of the ministry school I direct, Global School of Supernatural Ministry, and her testimony of healing and freedom that is in this book is being used by God to bring the same salvation, healing, and freedom throughout the earth. The engaging writing style and story sharing will draw you in to the power of God that restores and transforms any person who will say "Yes!" to Jesus. The author lives this truth through her life and releases it to others. Your life will experience this same power as you engage this book.

Dr. Mike Hutchings

Director of Education, Global Awakening School of Supernatural Ministry
President, God Heals PTSD Foundation
Mechanicsburg, PA

If there has been any recent writing on conversion experience and testimonies on the visible presence of God, the fiery touch of the Holy Spirit, the love of Christ, and a raw faith that activates the supernatural, it is practically in your hand. This book is interactive, explicit, and thought-provoking. I recommend it for personal devotion, Sunday school lessons, pastoral study, church worker's training, and believers desiring to pray and see miracles happen before their own eyes.

Suzanne Kutz, thanks for allowing God to use you to pen down this master class—*Jesus Shattered My Religion*. I have been sensing some demonic attacks. But your testimony of how Jesus instantly healed your horse jumped my faith into action. I said to myself, *if Jesus can heal a horse in the middle of the night, then what more about me created in His image and likeness?* I got free instantly. Hallelujah! Please read it prayerfully; you are the next in line for miracles. Amen.

Odysseus N. Gbor MA.

Founder/General Overseer and Lead Pastor Victory Center International Church, City of Faith Worldwide, Monrovia, Liberia, West Africa

In *Jesus Shattered My Religion*, Sue Kutz takes the reader on an intimate journey of truth. From harrowing survival to thriving advancement, her story has the fingerprints of the Savior and the evidence of the Kingdom. Yet her story is our story. No matter your family background, denominational history, income level, or educational achievements, you will quickly find similarities and hope in your relationship with Jesus Christ. On our quest to be like Jesus and reign in His victory, this book reminds readers of the powerful invitation of healing, heart restoration, and the promises Jesus has for each of us. Kutz's encounters with heaven through present-day miracles will leave you renewed in your understanding that Jesus is alive today. With deep biblical knowledge and practical tips, *Jesus Shattered My Religion* will be an essential cornerstone in every disciple's library.

Megan Schreiber

Author, Speaker, Founder Harvest Consulting

I first met Sue at the Global Conference at Community of Nations in Brazil, and we immediately connected. She went back to the United States, but our friendship got stronger as we connected on video calls to share Jesus and the amazing things the Holy Spirit, our friend and teacher, was showing both of us. *Jesus Shattered My Religion* made me cry, laugh, and see myself in so many experiences Sue had as the Father showed her how He loved her and how to relate to Him deeper and deeper.

It is so encouraging to read Sue's pursuit for answers and for connection. I relate to her in so many ways, and I witness the signs and wonders God is continually doing in her life. Even through the most excruciating loss and pain, the Father was there listening and speaking to her.

Sue is an extraordinary storyteller. She has a unique manner of telling her encounters with God that captivated me as a child listening to a fairy tale. I love how she paints the words and presents such vivid images. I was totally immersed in her life journey as she invited us to ride with her, showing us the road map of trust and confidence God initiated with her. Telling her own story with God, Sue shakes our possible religious strongholds with such grace. I strongly recommend reading this life-changing book. You will realize that the same God who changed Sue's life forever can and will do the same for you.

Marcia Godinho
Translator, Brasilia, Brazil

In *Jesus Shattered My Religion*, Sue introduces the Jesus she walks with, talks with, laughs with, dances with, and loves with her whole heart, soul, mind, and strength every day. It is the story and testimony of how this "lover-bird" woman shares Jesus' love with the world. She has devoted the last ten years of her life to sharing her time, energy, and the soul-winning love of Jesus Christ with the world. Although I tend to minister with boldness and fervor, Sue's voice always echoes in my mind, "Do it with love, sister, always do it with love." This book will show you the beauty of what real love can do in a life and what the redeeming love of Jesus Christ has waiting for you too.

No S. Ringer
Vice President, Commercial Relationship Manager
Susquehanna Community Bank

From hell on this earth in Pennsylvania to eternity in this world and the next in God's house, this is a true story. I witnessed Sue go through many of the stages described in this book but never had all the details until now.

God, through His Son, our Savior Jesus, is in control of all our lives. We just need the faith of a mustard seed to turn our lives over to Him. We just need to ask and then live our lives according to His direction because He already knows our destination here on earth and our final eternal destiny.

Jesus Shattered My Religion is not written by Sue alone. Through Jesus and the Holy Spirit, God's thoughts within Sue are just pouring out of her in this book like a fast-flowing river. This is God's purpose for Sue at this time and, thus, the book. He wants all to know that faith and belief in His Son, Jesus, far outweigh any of the man-made religions. Different religions might lead you on a path to find God, but you find God personally. God wants to save and love you and me!

In a way, Sue is the result of several miracles both inside and outside of her. After many years of trauma, abuse, and heartache, she was saved to experience God's love through His Son, Jesus Christ. A completely broken soul revived! Brought back to life to love and live again!

Through baptism by immersion in a lake, Sue received the Holy Spirit and now can share the story, hers and Theirs (the Three in One), with all of us. God chose Sue to write this book so that all who read it and talk to others about it might experience the same faith and belief in God. "For God so loved the world that he gave His only Son, that whoever believes in Him shall not perish but have eternal life" (John 3:16). Amen.

Col. (USAF, Ret) Robert Phillips
State College, PA

Whether written or spoken, a testimony has great power. There is something about the Christian witness that speaks to the soul of a person, and God is always glorified when we share the story of Jesus Christ in our own lives. Suzanne is giving her personal testimony in this book.

Sue is my spiritual mentor, and she has quite the story to tell. This book speaks to just part of her life—the part which sets the stage for anyone who desires proof that God truly does exist. I recommend this book to anyone who is seeking to know if

God is real. Suzanne has declared how God continues to work in her life, as well as in the lives of all His children. This book gives me hope for the future as Suzanne shares how the Father continues to move in our world today. As a pastor, I highly recommend this book to anyone searching for God's existence in the lives of ordinary people.

God is the author of Sue's story, and her story is a must-read for everyone seeking to know Jesus Christ as their personal Savior. The Holy Spirit dictated this book to Sue, and she has spent countless hours deliberately making sure she is faithful to write down every word given as they are Spirit-filled.

Senior Pastor Ken Brown
Noxen, Alderson & Kunkle United Methodist Churches
Susquehanna Conference, PA

I am delighted to recommend the book *Jesus Shattered My Religion*. It is a magnificent narrative of a modern-day, miracle-working God written in a captivating, hope-infused manner, to the point, and practical for ministry. I met Sue early in the process of God's uniquely tailored "do-over." I watched God sovereignly do a beautiful transformational work in her life. It was truly amazing and a privilege to be up close and personal to watch God work. The process of transformation and empowerment in Sue's life continues for His unfathomable glory and as part of God's marvelous story of redemption and love put in place before the beginning of time, ultimately culminating in a new heaven and a new earth!

Janet Madore
Intercessor and scribe to several of Sue's heavenly encounters

Acknowledgments

- As mentioned in this book's dedication, I owe all thanks to **the Holy Spirit** for the continual inspiration and leading through this entire book. I literally did not know what was coming in each chapter until I heard it from Him. He led me every step of the way, masterfully weaving my testimony with Christian theology and scriptural reference and helping me to work through my own eschatological beliefs that I might be ready in season and out of season to give an account for them. Through Him, I have encountered God in such full living manifestation and most especially for being the source conduit of my abiding union with Jesus Christ.

- My dear "twin" sister, **Susan Oh**, who tearfully pleaded with me to write my testimony and loving encounters with Jesus immediately upon the finishing of my initial suicide prevention book. It was her heartfelt plea that spurred me to write again and her continual encouragement that kept me soldiering on through the months that followed. She was my most avid cheerleader. She also witnessed first-hand the incredible encounters that I experienced in Brazil both in 2018 and 2019 and prayed with me through both the trials and the triumphs of those mission trips.

- **Col. Robert Phillips, USAF, Retired** and **Mrs. Robert Phillips**, for walking alongside my daughters and me through my husband's death and my journey of discovering my Lord and Savior, Jesus Christ. They held us all together when we thought we could not take one more step. "Colonel

Bob" was there on the worst day of my life, and he was the surrogate father who walked my daughter down the aisle at her wedding. Friends like that don't grow on trees. We are all indebted for your friendship, kindness, love, and unfailing support through the last 11 years.

- **Pastor Kenneth Brown**, who covered this book in prayer nearly every single day of its writing, which spanned hundreds of hours. His tireless prayers helped me battle through thousands of literary challenges. His supportive listening ear encouraged me through countless writing trials. He kept the enemy at bay, and the spiritual communication lines up, running, and crystal clear.

- My dear sister in ministry, **No Ringer**, who relentlessly and valiantly prayed every day for me, my health, revelation, fortitude, conviction to finish, and just about everything else a person could want to be covered in prayer. Her fearless and fierce prayers blessed me in every conceivable way. Her unwavering, steadfast, and unshakable encouragement pushed me to excellence so that I might glorify Jesus to the best of my ability, for He is worthy of all honor, glory, and praise.

- My dear friends, **Wendy Ware** and **Ann Skotek**, who reviewed my writing for biblical and grammatical accuracy, sentence structure, and ease of reading, always with a kind eye for the unchurched who needed the scriptural references to many of my vastly abbreviated Bible story synopses. Their tenacious editing was a huge asset in the overall production of this book.

- To **the myriad of friends, family, and fellow Christian ministers** who supported me, cheered me on, and prayed for me as I completed two books back to back in 12 months. Thank you one and all!

Contents

"Take my yoke upon you and learn from me,

for I am gentle and humble in heart,

and you will find rest for your souls.

For my yoke is easy and my burden is light."

Matthew 11:29-30 NIV

When my "twin sister" Sue said that the Lord nudged her to write her book, *Jesus Shattered My Religion*, I was ecstatic! I was so excited about the world meeting the God she encounters daily. When she asked me to write the Foreword, my heart rejoiced, as this is truly an honor like no other.

In 2017, I met Sue at the *Supernatural Life Conference* hosted by Life Center Church in Harrisburg, Pennsylvania. She knows, that she knows, that she knows that Jesus is real because she meets Him daily in spirit. To her, Jesus is not an imaginary figure that we are to just praise and worship. Jesus is no longer someone she only reads about in the Bible in order to attain some imaginary eternal life. Jesus is more REAL to her than someone standing right in front of her. For Sue, the Bible comes alive through encounters with Jesus, which compels her to share Jesus with the world by taking the next bold and courageous steps in full obedience to Him. Since 2010, this is the story of her life, and she has been persistent, relentless, and fierce in her pursuit of Jesus, no matter the cost. She is incredibly humble, yet she walks in the full authority that God has given her through His sacrifice. As she prays in the name of Jesus, she has seen broken hearts and bodies healed, the lost delivered from darkness, and prisoners of the enemy of our souls set free.

Her prophetic gifting is nothing short of astonishing. For many around the world, her releasing of God's prophetic words catapults His children into their predestined callings. These words are extremely accurate and filled with His love. I have been one of the most blessed beneficiaries of her prophetic anointing.

Sue is a living testimony of the miracle and wonder of God. Her passion for the Lord is truly beyond admirable. Despite the unimaginable obstacles she has endured for decades, her life has been completely redeemed, restored, and transformed by opening her heart to receive God's grace. She lives as a victor, not as a victim—as a leader, not as a follower—and as a daughter of the King of kings, not as a lost widow. She lives a life of full freedom in full surrender to the Lord. Out of that real, deep love and joy-filled relationship with our Lord, she has learned to hear His voice clearly and courageously obey His guidance. I know there is nothing she would not do for the Lord.

The song by Chris Tomlin titled *"Is He Worthy?¹"* is playing in my heart as I am writing this.

Is He worthy? Is He worthy?
Of all blessing and honor and glory.
Is He worthy of all this?
(He is)
Does the Father truly love us?
(He does)
Does the Spirit move among us?
(He does)
And ... More

How true! Is He worthy of all our praise, all of our hearts, minds, souls, and strength? He is! Is He worthy to lay our lives down completely and take His yoke upon us and follow His ways? He is!

I am a fourth generation Christian who, in 2012, asked the question, "What is the purpose of my life?" Since then, Jesus has been faithful in answering that question, and indeed every question, that has come. He has put me on the trajectory of a joy-filled life beyond my wildest dreams or that I ever thought possible for any human being. I now know that "With God, all things are possible" (Matthew 19:26 NIV).

---

1 *"Is He Worthy?"* Contemporary Christian worship song first released October 26, 2018 on the Holy Roar studio album sung by Chris Tomlin, produced by Ed Cash and Brian Fowler and written by Andrew Peterson and Ben Shive. Retrieved from https://en.wikipedia.org/wiki/Holy_Roar_(album). Accessed 1 July 2021.

Are you thirsty to know why He created you? This book beautifully weaves Sue's personal testimonies of God's goodness and faithfulness to reveal a personal God. The God who knows everything about us and yet still pursues us with His abounding love and says, "Let Me help you... let Me love you... let Me share My truth about you... let Me free you from the bondage of the enemy. Would you believe that in Me you can overcome all things? Would you believe that you can go from strength to strength, faith to faith, and victory to victory in Me? Would you believe there is nothing I cannot redeem and restore? Would you open your hearts to hear My voice to guide your every step? Would you be willing to walk a life of faith in Me and not by your own plan? Would you believe all My promises? Would you receive ALL that I have for you? From the abundance of My love, would you share that love with the world, not by your strength or power but by the power of the Holy Spirit?" Let your answer be Yes! Yes! Yes! Because your yes frees you, frees us all, to choose the giver of life, the only giver of life in this world, Jesus. I assure you that your life will never be the same.

> *The God who knows everything says, "Let Me love you ..."*

If you picked up this book, I hope and trust that you open your heart and receive its message of hope. This is truly a life-changing book. It is written in an easy, conversational style, as if you are talking with a friend. I also hope you will be compelled to share this book with your loved ones. His love is uncontainable. We cannot help but to share His love as it overflows from us like Niagara Falls. I have begun to say, "No regrets only expect!" that the good Lord awaits to bless you. He truly loves you beyond your wildest imagination.

This is my prayer for every one of you.

> "I pray that He would unveil within you the unlimited riches of His glory and favor until supernatural strength floods your innermost being with His divine might and explosive power. Then, by constantly using your faith, the life of Christ will be released deep inside you, and the resting place of His love will become the very source and root of your life. Then you will be empowered to discover what every holy one experiences—the great magnitude of the astonishing love of Christ in all its dimensions.
>
> How deeply intimate and far-reaching is His love! How enduring and inclusive it is! Endless love beyond measurement that transcends our understanding— this extravagant love pours into you until you are filled to overflowing with the fullness of God!
>
> Never doubt God's mighty power to work in you and accomplish all this. He will achieve infinitely more than your greatest request, your most unbelievable dream, and exceed your wildest imagination! He will outdo them all, for His miraculous power constantly energizes you. Now we offer up to God all the

glorious praise that rises from every church in every generation through Jesus Christ—and all that will yet be manifest through time and eternity. Amen!" (Ephesians 3:16-21 TPT).

–Susan E. Oh

Investment Director of the Pennsylvania
Public School Employees' Retirement System
Korea Leader of the Global Apostolic Prayer Network

Chapter 1

Rescued

Hope to Hang Onto

This book is a story of freedom from mindsets that may be holding you imprisoned to lies and deceptions into a renewed mind that delights in happiness, peace, and joy. It is possible, and I'm here to say that if it could happen for me, it can happen for you too. Believe me when I say that I'm living proof that a life of sustained joy is possible, and I want to share what I have learned the hard way, so you don't have to travel that same painful road and get there so much more quickly and easily. To literally provide you with a roadmap for the paths to take and the ones to avoid and to point out where the potholes, pitfalls, and danger zones are located.

This book is about recognizing an infinitely loving God who wants to bless you with every good and wonderful blessing from heaven. It's about Jesus and how He makes a way for us here and now to be set free and live the abundant life He paid in full for us. It's about learning what promises God has made us and how to remove Satan from your life before he has a chance to steal, kill, and destroy it[1] for you. It's learning that we live both a physical life and a spiritual one at the same time and our choices determine what happens in that life, both good and bad.

I'm stopping for the "one." I'm leaving the ninety-nine and looking for the lost one.[2] The one who has become so entangled they can't break free on their own; for the one who can't see any light at the end of their tunnel. I'm stopping for you! Let me help free you from the shackles that may have held you bound for years and years.

I want to introduce you to the God that changes fear into confidence, pain into comfort, suffering into relief, depression into happiness, heartache into love. I want to introduce you to a God that changes worry into delight, bitterness into gladness, and torment into contentment. I want to introduce you to a God that changes mercilessness to grace, powerlessness into authority, and imprisonment into freedom. That is the God that took me from the edge of destruction to an abundant life of happiness and joy beyond my wildest imagination. I don't know what you may currently think about God or Jesus or any religious belief, but I want to introduce you to the Jesus that suddenly walked into my life and changed everything that I

---

[1] John 10:10 ESV "The thief comes only to steal and kill and destroy. I came that they may have life and have it abundantly."

[2] Matthew 18:12 NLT "If a man has a hundred sheep and one of them wanders away, what will he do? Won't he leave the ninety-nine others on the hills and go out to search for the one that is lost?"

have ever thought or believed about God, a Savior, or heaven and hell. When He steps into your life, light always comes in, and help is available for every single problem you have—bar none!

I want to walk you through how things that happen in your life have both a physical and a spiritual side to them, and as you understand how each side influences the other, you can take back control of your life and change the trajectory of where your life is heading. I want to help you start to see how things that have happened in your life do not dictate your future and that they do not define the ultimate goals you set for your life. I want to offer you some knowledge to help dispel some of the lies you may be believing about yourself and give you a clearer picture of your true identity. I want to help you transform your life by transforming the things you believe about what is possible when you partner with God. Spoiler alert: All things are possible with God!

Where Are You?

If you have picked up this book, you are more than likely looking for some help to get free from where you are to some other place, most likely a happier place. You may be in a very dark, desperate place and really need help, or you may just want to help someone you love or care about. Regardless of where you are right now, I want to show you the way. As a matter of fact, I want to show you how to find the way, the truth, and the light. I want to share with you how I found my way from the pit of despair to the light of hope, from bone-gnawing grief to ecstatic joy, from utter defeat to triumphant victory, and from total brokenness to fully restored wholeness.

I have come to realize that writing a book is a process-plain and simple. A process of distilling information down to tell a story or give instruction or direction. A process of taking you from one point or place to another. It is very much like mapping out directions for a trip or finding your way from one end of the mall to the other. You look for the arrow that says, "YOU ARE HERE," and then search the map or floor plan for where you want to go or end up. That is exactly the process that I want to show you in the fewest miles or steps to get you from where you are now to where you want to be. A process that doesn't take a GPS or cartographer to figure out how to get there. This book is just such a roadmap to take you from where you are today, what has happened to you up to this day, through the lies that have stained your vision, to the truth of who you really are, to the one and only path you will ever need to walk on again…ever! If that sounds like a trip you'd like to take, then buckle yourself in, and let's get going.

Jesus is Your Lifeline

So who exactly is this Savior, Jesus Christ? Well, He has lots of titles. He is also known as the Prince of Peace, the King of kings, the Messiah, and the Anointed One, but most importantly, He is known as the Son of God. Christianity has a veritable plethora of titles and names for Him, but I want to introduce you to the Jesus I met in a radical encounter over ten years ago and not just the one from the pages of a religious book. He is all of the things the Holy Bible talks about but so, so much more. It's also worth noting that Christianity is a religion, but I don't want to teach you religion; I want to help you build a relationship with the best friend there ever was or that you will ever have. To come to know the one who changed my entire life with just a whisper. To the one who is standing ready to do the exact same thing for you.

I'm going to start with my first encounter with God the Father and Jesus Christ when everything first changed for me—when the fear of God turned into the overwhelming love of God, when Jesus stepped into my life and opened the pages of the most amazing love story I've ever known. So let me begin to paint the amazing story for you of how Jesus put the pieces of my shattered life back together even more beautifully than they had ever been before. However, this story doesn't start out exactly in love, joy, and bliss. For God to put the pieces back together again, it first had to be shattered. Sometimes we do the shattering ourselves; sometimes, others do the shattering for us. Mine was the latter. My life came crashing down four months prior to the incredible entrance of Jesus into my world when my husband committed suicide. That event brings everyone's life to an abrupt halt, and life as you knew it ceases to exist. The ground falls away under your feet, and your mind goes numb. You can't put two thoughts together, and you have no idea how you will recover from the shock wave that this act has sent through your life and the lives of your family. Devastation doesn't really describe what happens to you when someone commits suicide because that only describes what people see on the outside. But what happens on the inside of those left behind is far more despicable and destructive.

It is a pain that doesn't stop getting worse and devours your insides till you feel completely and totally empty, void, and barren. There is a nothingness that still eats at your insides and torments your mind. It is unrelenting, unstoppable, and unyielding. It takes you to such a dark place that you cannot see any light or hope. Ironically it is said that the sign over the gates of hell reads: "Enter here all who have no hope." Time literally stands still as the world rushes by, and you can't stop the madness of it all. You can't go back, and you can't move forward. Everything comes to a screeching halt.

If I had had a relationship with Jesus instead of just the fear of God back then, I would have known that Jesus offers us a whole different way to live; to live in peace, joy, and love. That the life I was living was not what He had planned for me. It's not what He has planned for any of us. It's not the way we have to live, and there is a way out. That, my friends, is what this book is all about. The way out of the nightmare life you or your loved one may be living. The way towards the light that gives freedom and hope. The light that gives freedom from the inside out.

As Paul Harvey used to say, "And now for the rest of the story."[3] Thank heavens my story didn't end there. Thank heavens that God interrupted my life and changed everything I ever knew about who God was, is, and always will be. Thank God

---

[3] Aurandt (Harvey, Jr.), *Paul Paul Harvey's The Rest of the Story* (New York: Bantam Books, 1984) Retrieved from: https://en.wikipedia.org/wiki/The_Rest_of_the_Story. Accessed 15 June 2021.

He showed up one day and changed the rest of my life forever. He entered in and destruction exited; it wasn't overnight, but it did happen. What I learned in the next ten years is what I want to tell you in a few short pages. I want to tell you about how my life did a 180° turnaround and found a never-ending joy that is waiting for you too.

About four months after my husband died, my younger daughter went into a terrible depression and asked me if I could spend some time with her. She was in graduate school, about eight hours away from me. So I planned a short, mini-vacation at a lovely hotel a few hours south of her college. God knows I needed a time out from the nightmare I was living, so I was happy for the time to get away from it all for a while. Unfortunately, instead of me lifting my daughter out of her depression, I fell into an even deeper depression myself. I cried night and day for two days. I was inconsolable, but I went out on the balcony that overlooked the bay on the morning of the third day and prayed to God to help me. Well, truth be told, it wasn't exactly a prayer. I was so hurt and angry I yelled at God and shook my fist at heaven, defying God to do something, anything! I defied Him to show me how He was going to make good out of this situation and vehemently declared that I was not going to get off that balcony until He told me something to help me recover my life so that I could face the world again.

God delivered! Wow, did He deliver! Suddenly I fell to the balcony floor and was shaking violently when I heard the voice of God audibly! His voice came out of everything! Out of the air, out of the ground, out of the water, out of the buildings, even out of my own body! Every cell in my body was vibrating wildly. His voice boomed in the air, "DO NOT PUT THE LORD YOUR GOD TO THE TEST!" There was no denying it was God and a true fear of the Lord came over me. I have never been more shaken to my core than at that very moment. God was talking out loud to me! Trust me when I say that I knew the power of God that day. I have never been the same since.

There was no denying it was God, and a true fear of the Lord came over me

Then I saw a beautiful white bird appear in the sky out of nowhere. It glided through the air without ever flapping its wings even once and landed on the far end of my balcony railing. An amazing peace came over me, and I thought out loud, "That must be the Holy Spirit." As silly as this may sound, I actually expected that bird to talk to me, but it didn't; however, Jesus did. For the first time in my life, I heard Jesus speaking. The most profound peace and love I had ever experienced enveloped me, and in one precious moment, my whole world of pain and sorrow stood still. All fear left me as Jesus' perfect love[4] washed away everything but His tremendous love for me.

Gently, lovingly and ever so reassuringly, He whispered into my heart and spirit. He told me about all the wonderful things I was going to do with Him and all the incredible things He was going to do through me. Love and joy like I had never

[4] 1 John 4:18 GNT "There is no fear in love; perfect love drives out all fear. So then, love has not been made perfect in anyone who is afraid, because fear has to do with punishment."

known flooded my spirit, and an unquenchable hope rose up from deep within my heart and very soul. Parts of my being that had never known true love were awakened and enlightened in a marvelous swirl of deep emotion. Jesus touched the very essence of who I was and who I was created to be. My spirit knew my Creator, and recognized an unfathomable love that my mind could scarcely comprehend. My spirit experienced the fullness of perfect love, perfect joy, perfect peace, perfect everything. In those first moments of bliss, the entirety of who I was transcended the physical world, and all that I had ever known was possible.

There was a tenderness and understanding that permeated right into my bones. There was a desire to know and be known. There was an utter unconditional acceptance of who I was. There was a gentleness that soothed every anxiety or concern. There was a goodness and purity of intent. There was total contentment of space and time. There was a sense of complete trust and safety. It was as if the whole world just came to a stop and was held in perfect stillness. I was captivated and totally apprehended by a love that reached in and touched every part of me and every part of everything that ever was or will be. To say it was completely surreal barely scratches the surface of what I was experiencing.

I now knew there was a love so much greater than anything that existed in the physical world. There existed a love that no human words could adequately describe or portray. There was a loving God that I had never met, and His love outweighed every problem, every disappointment, and every crushing pain that I had ever borne. There was a God of unimaginable love that no one ever told me about. There was a God of such magnitude of power that nothing in this world could possibly match or equate to. There was a God of such complexity and completeness this world could not contain or explain Him. There was a God that superseded everything known to man. There was a God of such utter magnificence all thoughts of this world ceased to matter. Nothing in all the world could compare.

To say this was all mind-boggling would be a tremendous understatement. I was totally and utterly overwhelmed with what was happening to me. I wasn't sure if I was having a nervous breakdown or just plain losing my mind or if I had died and actually gone to heaven. I have no idea to this day just how long this encounter actually lasted, but I do know unequivocally that I never wanted it to end. I would have gladly stayed in that love embrace for the rest of eternity. That encounter with the living God changed everything for me forever.

When this amazingly marvelous encounter ended, shaken and bewildered, I staggered back into the hotel room literally hanging onto the hotel walls for support. I explained to my daughter through a jumble of tears, confusion, and bliss what had just happened. Among all the incredible things Jesus told me that morning, He told me to remember Jeremiah 29:11. At that time, I had absolutely no idea that it was a Bible verse. The only Jeremiah I knew was a bullfrog in a 70's song. I didn't even know 29:11 represented a chapter and verse in the Bible.

I just knew that Jesus said it was important and that I should remember it. So my daughter Googled Jeremiah 29:11, and this is what she read to me: "For I know the plans I have for you, declares the LORD, plans to prosper you and not to harm you, plans to give you hope and a future" (NIV). I fell to my knees, flooded in a torrent of tears. I had indeed gotten a message from God! He had not abandoned me nor forsaken[5] me. He had spoken directly to me in the most phenomenal way and given me an invincible hope to soldier on into the tremendously uncertain future, assured that He would be right there to help me. Ironically the actual title of that 70's song with Jeremiah the bullfrog was Joy to the World.[6] Coincidence? I think not.

To say my life changed that day would fall woefully short of the transformation that happened to me that day. I was completely overwhelmed at the very thought that the God of all the universe had spoken out loud to me! He was real, and He was very much alive. He had heard my prayer and answered it beyond my wildest imagination. He proved Himself to be faithful to His word. He stepped into the shambles of my life and changed everything. Every Bible story of God speaking to people I could ever remember suddenly became real to me in the most astonishing and utterly undeniable fashion. God was

---

[5] Deuteronomy 31:6 NIV "Be strong and courageous. Do not be afraid or terrified because of them, for the LORD your God goes with you; He will never leave you nor forsake you."

[6] Hoyt Axton, "Joy to the World" Three Dog Night originally released the song on their fourth studio album, Naturally, in November 1970, and subsequently released an edited version of the song as a single in February 1971.(Three Dog Night at American Recording Company, 1970) Retrieved from: https://en.wikipedia.org/wiki/Joy_to_the_World_(Three_Dog_Night_song); Accessed 15 June 2021.

real! God is real! And His unmeasurably loving plans are to prosper me and to prosper you. The future He has planned for all of us contains immense hope, love, assurance, forgiveness, peace, security, and every other good and perfect thing, and it's yours and mine for the taking.

In the ten years that have passed since that holy, blessed encounter I have devoted myself to getting to know that loving God and developing an ever-growing, loving relationship with Jesus Christ. To learning everything that I can about who He is, who He was, and who He wants to be for me. I have done countless Bible studies and read everything I could get my hands on about people encountering God. I have researched different religious beliefs about God and what various faith churches believe God wants from us. I have studied the Hebrew culture and how it applies to Christianity. I learned about the supernatural world and manifestations of the Holy Spirit, as well as the demonic forces that exist. I learned about spiritual realms that I never knew actually existed. I learned how they functioned and the rules that apply to those realms. I learned how what happens on earth affects heaven and how what happens in the heavenly realm affects the earth. But most importantly of all, I learned that Jesus loves us with an everlasting, all-powerful, and consuming love. I learned that His shed blood on the cross at Calvary bought us eternal salvation and freedom.

Christianity 101

As a writer, I will readily testify to you that the English language, or pretty much any known earthly language for that matter, cannot adequately describe this Jesus with human words. He transcends description or explanation so telling you about Him is a bit stifling and complicated. The vastness of who He is supersedes our possible understanding, so I will be forced to give you a bit of a Christianity 101 mixed in to explain who He is. But above all, I want to explain who He is to me, thereby explaining how I got from where I was to where I am now because of a relationship like no other. Ultimately bringing Him from just words on a page to a living, loving, miracle-working reality in your life.

So here goes my very best *Reader's Digest*[7] version of Christianity. Christianity is the belief that Jesus Christ is the Son of God and the salvation He offers us is for all eternity. Following the life example Christ modeled for us and living according to His teachings is known as Christianity or, more simply, the act of being Christ-like. Christianity has its roots in the Hebrew heritage and faith in the one true God, Yahweh. Christianity believes that God is a Triune being with three spiritual persons comprising a Triune Godhead consisting of God, the Father; Jesus Christ, the Son; and the Holy Spirit. It further believes that God is the all-powerful Creator of everything ever created, including mankind, angels, all living creatures, and the universe. There are hundreds of more pages in the Holy Bible referred to as the Old Testament that goes

---

[7] *Reader's Digest* is an American general-interest family magazine, published 12 times a year. Formerly based in Pleasantville, New York, it is now headquartered in midtown Manhattan. The magazine was founded in 1922 by DeWitt Wallace and Lila Bell Wallace. For many years, Reader's Digest was the best-selling consumer magazine in the United States. It was known for it's condensed and concise writing format. Retrieved from Wikipedia: https://en.wikipedia.org/wiki/Reader%27s_Digest; Accessed 3 January 2021.

into great length explaining the beginnings of the Hebrew faith, but for now, it will suffice to know that God is the Father, located in heaven, Jesus Christ is God's Son who also came to earth and lived a human life example for us to follow and a bit later in this book, there will be more explanation regarding who the Holy Spirit is in the Triune-Godhead.

I learned these basics as I attended parochial school[8] from first through eighth grades. I never questioned the fact that God was God or that He had a Son named Jesus that He sent down to earth to help us figure out how to behave so we could eventually go back to heaven and live with God again forever in carefree bliss. The stories were simple enough, and everyone I knew in my little life all believed these same things, so I accepted them without question. For what it is worth, I still believe them, but in the last ten years, I've asked a lot more questions! Since I am now 60 plus years old, that was a very long time ago, and Christianity was taught in a very different way. The old way of teaching the Christian religion was to instill the fear of God's judgment and the potential for being sent to hell instead of heaven for an eternity of living in unquenchable burning fire. Even a six-year-old mentality could reason that bliss was better than burning. But as is often the case, when the pendulum swings too far to one end or the other things can get extreme.

---

[8] "Parochial school" A parochial school is a private primary or secondary school affiliated with a religious organization, and whose curriculum includes general religious education in addition to secular subjects, such as science, mathematics and language arts. The word parochial comes from the same root as 'parish', and parochial schools were originally the educational wing of the local parish church. Retrieved from: https://en.wikipedia.org/wiki/Parochial_school Access: 4 August 2021.

Fear was the medium of choice for forced behavioral adherence rather than instilling an unconditional love comprehension. As I grew, the pendulum swung further and further toward an ultimate demise in hell and a perception that heaven was more than likely unattainable for such a sinner as myself. My youthful understanding of God had nothing to do with love and certainly not unconditional love but rather was seeped in the fearful wrath of God. I tell you this for several reasons. One is that you, too, may have been taught that God is an angry and vengeful God, or you may believe you have fallen too far to be redeemed, but I assure you that neither is correct. Also to help you understand the massive difference between what I was taught and believed and the immensely different encounter I had with the second person of the Godhead, Jesus Christ.

Shattering My Religion

My radical encounter with the three persons of the Triune Godhead shattered everything I had ever learned or believed about my Christian religion. You could say it literally blew it to smithereens. I was now faced with the dilemma of deciding for myself which one was right. The angry and punishing God or the immensely loving Jesus I'd just encountered. The one thing that I knew beyond a shadow of a doubt was that the loving one was more real to me than anything I had ever encountered up to that point in my life. I also had an all-consuming, burning desire to draw closer to that God than I ever knew was possible. I simply could not get enough of that immeasurably intoxicating love. So began my search to understand what exactly had happened to me on that amazing morning and what in the world I was now going to believe about the religion I had been living for fifty years of my life up to that day.

I'd like to tell you that I figured out early on that God wasn't a religion, but that just wouldn't be true. I circled around and around, trying to put something concrete under my old belief system because I literally had nothing to stand on for quite a while. I went to my parish priest, I queried pastors of my friends, I talked with my church's Spiritual Director, and I'm not especially proud of the fact that I actually had to go out and buy a Bible to try and find some answers. Ultimately, however, I was still in the same quandary. The God of religion was not the God I met in my encounter. Finally, the bells went off, ding, ding, ding, God isn't religion! Hallelujah! I now had an answer and a few thousand new questions to boot.

The God of religion was not the God I met in my encounter

Was everything I was taught a lie? How was it possible that I missed the loving Jesus all this time? Is the angry God still up there? Why didn't I ever hear Jesus loves me? Do the Ten Commandments still exist? Why did the nuns scare me half to death about God's judgment and going to hell? What was this burning inside me for this newfound God? Who, what, where, why, how questions poured forth until I was totally, completely, and thoroughly exhausted. The more answers I got, the more questions there were. This was becoming a vicious cycle until I had another epiphany. I'm not going to find the answers in religion or what

I had known up to that point. I was going to have to go to Jesus, the source of that crazy, radical love, and ask Him for some answers. That is how my relationship with the living God began. I didn't know it at the time, but I was beginning the friendship, not only of a lifetime but for eternity.

A New Perspective

I needed to analyze this new perspective that I was suddenly privy to. I had to figure out how to get in touch with this loving Jesus. How exactly do you call Him back up again? Pretty sure He was out of my calling area. You would think this would be a pretty easy thing to do, considering I had been praying all my life. I knew how to send up the prayer, but I just never expected that an audible answer would come back down. I don't know what I was actually expecting that day on the balcony, but it sure wasn't the audible voice of God! Honestly, that part was still pretty scary, so I didn't want to get the lines crossed with Him again. I wanted to connect to Jesus' extension for sure. As I write this, it all now sounds pretty funny, but I just didn't know that prayer could be a two-way communication. I knew that there were people in the Bible who heard and talked with God, but that was a very select, holy group of saints, and I wasn't in their club, and as far as I knew, no one currently living was actually hearing from God. I will confess that there were many times that I wondered if I had really had a nervous breakdown, and this was all just a mental delusion I was now living in. The fear of God that had been drilled into me day after day, year after year, was still dominating my thought process. I truly did not want to make Him any angrier than He already was, but I could not escape the nagging hunger in my heart for more of that incredible love. That desire overcame my fear and drove me to keep seeking Jesus.

I ran over and over in my head exactly what I had said or prayed that day and in the days immediately proceeding my God encounter. What were the perfect words to pray and call Jesus back up? Did I have to go through several days and nights of crying again to reconnect? Did I need to go back to that same balcony and pray to successfully hear back from God? For all I knew, you only got one chance to talk with God, and that may have been it. There was no tent of meeting[9] where the Ark of the Covenant[10] was located anymore, so how then does this whole God-talking thing work? I wasn't a high priest or Moses or David or Mother Theresa or anybody to have the privilege to engage God in conversation. Finally, in my frustration, I just cried out, "Jesus, where are you?" And poof—He answered!

---

[9] Exodus 33:7 NLT "It was Moses' practice to take the Tent of Meeting and set it up some distance from the camp. Everyone who wanted to make a request of the LORD would go to the Tent of Meeting outside the camp."

[10] Hebrews 9:1-5 NLT "That first covenant between God and Israel had regulations for worship and a place of worship here on earth. [2]There were two rooms in that Tabernacle. In the first room were a lampstand, a table, and sacred loaves of bread on the table. This room was called the Holy Place. [3]Then there was a curtain, and behind the curtain was the second room called the Most Holy Place. [4]In that room were a gold incense altar and a wooden chest called the Ark of the Covenant, which was covered with gold on all sides. Inside the Ark were a gold jar containing manna, Aaron's staff that sprouted leaves, and the stone tablets of the covenant. [5]Above the Ark were the cherubim of divine glory, whose wings stretched out over the Ark's cover, the place of atonement."

"Yes, you did actually hear Me." He answered my questions before I even asked them. "No, you're not going crazy. Yes, it really is Me." I'd like to say that all my fears were washed away again in that moment, but I still wasn't convinced that I hadn't actually gone insane. Surely people were going to think that. Because the nice men in the white coats usually show up at your door when you start talking to people nobody can see. But Jesus didn't mind my disbelief; I'm guessing He gets a lot of that. He simply started talking to me in a voice that I could clearly hear in my head. Thankfully, it wasn't the booming audible voice that rattles your brain and lands you on the floor. Jesus simply, methodically, began to answer the hundreds of questions I just couldn't resist peppering Him with all over again. Amazingly, He had an answer for everything, and the only way I knew that I wasn't simply creating an imaginary person in my head was that each time He gave me an answer, He also told me where I could find the scripture or story in the Bible that verified the answer. Keep in mind that I hadn't had any Bible study up to this point other than the incredibly rudimentary principles I had learned in elementary school. So, I started my incredible journey of learning the Jesus side of the Bible; the "Yes Jesus loves me, this I know, cuz the Bible tells me so"[11] part of God. The part the nuns simply must have forgotten to mention so many years ago.

---

[11] "Jesus Loves Me" is a Christian hymn written by Anna Bartlett Warner (1827–1915). The lyrics first appeared as a poem in the context of an 1860 novel called *Say and Seal*, written by her older sister Susan Warner (1819–1885), in which the words were spoken as a comforting poem to a dying child. The tune was added in 1862 by William Batchelder Bradbury (1816–1868). Retrieved from https://en.wikipedia.org/wiki/Jesus_Loves_Me; Accessed 15 June 2021.

The next two years of my life were spent in experiencing a marvelous, awe-inspiring whirl of miracles, signs, and wonders with the lover of my soul, Jesus. Each morning I would wake up at 5:00 in the morning to talk with Jesus and learn from Him. Daily, Jesus would take me into actual heavenly encounters to experience the Bible stories I was just now truly learning. I continued to riddle Him with questions, and He answered them well beyond anything I could have imagined on my own, which kept me assured that I was actually hearing from God. Each day Jesus gave me the location in the Bible where I could find the scriptures that related to what we had talked about or I had experienced. I was amazed day after day that He could do that, never realizing that Jesus Himself was teaching me His marvelous story. Jesus was teaching me the Bible. I have to laugh at myself when I think about my child-like amazement that Jesus knew the Bible so well. He knew where everything was in there. Still makes me giggle whenever I think of it.

I also didn't have any concept that He was actually equipping me for the destiny that He had written for me before the beginning of time. His destiny for my life was, and is, far, far greater than anything I could have thought or imagined for myself. His destiny plan for you is too. So don't count yourself short because He's not done with you yet. As a matter of fact, this is just the beginning, and it just keeps getting better. Not everything is simple or without problems, but having someone who is always in your corner to help you no matter what may arise is really a terrific thing. It makes doing life a whole, whole lot easier. Having someone hold your hand and pick you up, or sometimes even drag you along, is what friends are for. It's what they do. It's what Jesus does for each and every one of us. You included! How He did that for me starting ten years ago, and is still doing it right up to this very day, is what I plan to share with you through this whole book. It may seem that I lived a charmed life, and right now, that would be true, but it wasn't always that way. As I touched on briefly at the very beginning of this book, my life wasn't always so happy. You will need to know some of my not-so-wonderful story as well to appreciate the fullness of the transformation that has taken place in my life. It is the testimony that I offer that actually brings Him glory—the amazing, extraordinary, astounding testimony of my life with "my" Jesus.

Crashed and Burned

So in sticking with my *Reader's Digest* version of storytelling, I want to give you a brief history of my life up to the day when my life suddenly crashed and burned. I was a good little Catholic girl. I was baptized as a baby, went to parochial school, received the sacraments of First Holy Communion and Confirmation, and was married in the Catholic church. I attended Mass every week, attended church on all the holy days of obligation, and raised both of my daughters in the Catholic religion. I lived a fairly normal life. I was married just after I had turned 20 years old to my childhood sweetheart. I was deeply in love with him, and everything seemed and looked perfectly normal. Life was certainly better since I had gotten out of my childhood home, where physical abuse and alcoholism were the norm. I never knew that everyone didn't get beaten on a regular basis, listen to daily screaming matches, or see their mother passed out drunk on the sofa. It was the only life I knew, and I accepted it as what normal daily life looked like.

My father was a huge, angry, and erratic man. He would become violent with little or no provocation. We, my three sisters and I, never knew what might set him off, but we knew that when that vein in his forehead started pulsating, we needed to run because someone was going to get a whipping. He would rip his belt off and start chasing us. That rage would end up with a belt whipping until either he wore out or one of us was bleeding. I was, more often than I care to remember, the target of his rage. The cause could simply have been that I forgot to put my hair up in a ponytail or because I talked at the dinner table, or God forbid I rolled my eyes at something that he said.

There was no love or parental nurturing in my home. I never even knew that existed. Never heard "I love you" or "good job." My mother never tended to us after the beatings or intervened in the beatings either. My sisters and I would huddle in the bathroom and cry as we examined the extent of our belt welts, black and blues, or bleeding. Our prayer of thanksgiving was when the buckle end of his belt had remained in his hand, sparing us even worse pain and bruising. We dared not make much noise, or a second round of whipping would be forthcoming, "so we had something to cry about." My mother drank herself into oblivion. Needless to say, she surely didn't want to endure that wrath either. To say that I had the fear of God beaten into me would by no means be an understatement.

Forced submission was a way of life for me. Children were to be seen and not heard. Mothering was a duty and necessity, not a joy or pleasure. The joy of the Lord was nowhere in my life of that you can be sure. Pretty sure I never even heard that phrase until much later in my adult life. Jesus loves you was not a concept that had ever been introduced in my life until many, many years later. So it should come as no surprise that I didn't recognize the abuse when it started in my married life.

I was young and vulnerable, but I was in love, or at least what I thought was love. I cherished this man who had saved me from the life of misery I had been living. He didn't beat me, and as a matter of fact, he just couldn't seem to get enough of me. The affection was so needed after an entire life of no tenderness whatsoever. I couldn't wait to bear his children and create the loving and caring family that I never had. He was brilliant, handsome, athletic, funny, charismatic, and generous. He had a great job and made a very good income. Life was grand ... until it wasn't.

I got pregnant with my first daughter about six months after we were married. It seemed like all my dreams were coming true until she came into the world two months prematurely. Back then, they didn't even call them "premies,"[12] and they didn't have special neonatal intensive care units at every hospital. She weighed less than five pounds, and she wasn't expected to live

---

[12] "Premies" Preterm birth, also known as premature birth, is the birth of a baby at fewer than 37 weeks gestational age, as opposed to full-term delivery at approximately 40 weeks. Retrieved from: https://en.wikipedia.org/wiki/Preterm_birth Accessed on 4 August 2021.

more than a few hours. But my pediatrician LifeFlighted[13] her to another medical center that had more advanced methods and equipment to help sustain her life. She did indeed fight for her little life, and several weeks later, we brought her home. She was so tiny and so helpless. Eventually, she was diagnosed with cerebral palsy and underwent numerous surgeries to correct the bodily functions that were adversely affected because of the bleeding in her brain at birth. She was a beautiful and loving child totally regardless of her constant physical struggles. My life became devoted to this tiny creature of both joy and pain.

My husband, however, delved into his work. He worked longer and longer hours and grew more and more distant from me. After a while, he stopped coming home at night and would stay overnight in the town where he now worked about an hour from our home. He would call me drunk in the middle of the night to tell me he wouldn't be coming home. Life was not looking so bright and shiny anymore. Eventually, there were other women that came and went from his life that drove a knife into my heart and into our marriage. I tried to mend the chasm in our marriage, but nothing I attempted would last for very long before the next round of fights and arguments ensued.

I'd love to tell you that my marriage had a storybook ending, but as you already know, it didn't. It played out like

___

[13] "LifeFlight," LifeFlight is an air ambulance service operated by Geisinger Health System in Pennsylvania, United States. Wikipedia; Retrieved from: https://en.wikipedia.org/wiki/Life_flight; Accessed 27 November 2020.

so many other marriages that you see on TV or in the movies. Desires, rejections, hurts, and pain, arguing and arguing some more. Clandestine meetings and phone calls, addictions and obsessions, mend-repair-break, mend-repair-break, the cycle was relentless and never-ending. We tried marriage counseling and therapy, but nothing worked. We rode an endless emotional rollercoaster that we just couldn't seem to get off, but I never thought that it would come to the screeching halt that it eventually did.

Thirty-two years later, I finally left my husband after things had spiraled totally out of control. His obsessions had become intolerable. His continually growing devotion to pornography, his drinking for hours at the local bar, his desire for other women, and his ever-accelerating compulsion for sex had become more than I could tolerate. It all culminated one night when I could not stop his advances. I could not stop him because he suddenly had the strength of a hundred men. The look in his eyes had changed to a sort of dead fish-eye look. They were glazed over and void of any expression, but the thing that scared me beyond anything I had ever experienced was the voice that came out from him. I say it that way because it was not his voice. It was entirely different, unworldly, and it made every hair on my body stand up. It was sinister and mean. Like nothing I had ever heard before.

It wasn't until many years later that I knew what it was that I had both witnessed and experienced that night. My husband had manifested demonically. He was no longer in control of himself; Satan was. He was no longer even aware of what he was doing or had done. Sadly, Satan is a remorseless taskmaster. He exacts his due and has no compunction on how that is paid or who gets hurt in the process. He has only one driving impetus; to steal, kill and destroy everything in his path. "The thief comes only to steal and kill and destroy" (John 10:10 NIV). He had stolen my beloved husband and destroyed our marriage, but he wasn't done yet.

After that horrific night, I left my husband and moved out into a safe house for fear of what my husband might do. He was no longer himself, and I literally feared for my life. It only took two months until the day I received the worst phone call anyone can ever receive. My husband had committed suicide. The world as I knew it had just come to that screeching halt. The worst possible outcome had happened, and there was absolutely nothing I could do to undo that fateful moment. That was the day my life suddenly crashed and burned. So when I tell you that I've been in that truly dark place where you don't see any light at the end of your tunnel and you are so exhausted you just don't want to try anymore, I'm not exaggerating. I had no idea how in the world I was going to pull the shattered pieces of my life back together again.

I needed a savior, but I didn't know Jesus back then. However, today I can say undeniably, that He was the only thing that saved me, and if you are anywhere near where I was, then you need a savior too. Jesus is undisputedly that Savior. I categorically believe that had my husband known Jesus back then, he wouldn't have had to die. He would have had a lifeline to pull him back from the edge of destruction. I'm throwing you that lifeline. Grab hold of it and never let go. I promise you Jesus will never let go of the other end, and He will rescue you from everything this life can throw at you.

This book is a culmination of trials, heartbreak, encounters, education, love, and restoration. I weave my personal stories, testimonies, and encounters with biblical scripture throughout the text to give you a more vivid account of the changes that happened in my life when Jesus entered into it and to bring to life what the Bible has been trying to teach us for the last two thousand years. Jesus is the answer to every question, problem, or issue that you will encounter in this lifetime, and the love that He has for us outweighs every single one of them. His love changes **everything**! Through the pages and stories that follow, I will explain who Jesus is and how His love was able to change my life forever and how it can change yours too if you let Him.

Jesus is the answer to every question,
problem, or issue that you will encounter
in this lifetime, and the love that He has for
us outweighs every single one of them.

Chapter 2

What Do You See?

Kintsugi

So how exactly do you go about putting the pieces of your life back together? Tough question, and undoubtedly countless books and theories have been written on the subject. My theory is that God actually puts us back together: "And we know that for those who love God all things work together for good, for those who are called according to His purpose" (Romans 8:28, ESV). God makes us even better than we were before our lives were shattered.

As I contemplated the many places in my life that were broken and Jesus' perfect process of restoring me to something even more beautiful because of the scars I bear, I thought of the amazing correlation of that process to the 15th-century ceramic repair process known as Kintsugi[1] (kint-su-gee). Japanese artisans were commissioned to repair priceless pieces of exquisite pottery using gold dust and lacquer, thus creating a one-of-a-kind work of art. Instead of gold dust and lacquer, God uses love, patience, and mercy. He polishes our brokenness with forgiveness and grace. Jesus tenderly leads us from brokenness back to wholeness, not perfection, but stronger than when we started because of the journey.

He creates an even more profound beauty and strength in us to weather life's storms. Storms that damage our minds, bodies, and hearts. Storms that bruise our feelings and our very spirits. We can make so many possible choices through our lives that don't always lead to opportune endings but rather to more brokenness, often leaving us in a heap of despair. But when we allow God to work His repair process in us, He takes our wreckage and creates something vastly more beautiful, valuable, and celebrated. God offers us a way back to an even more productive life in spite of our scars. Our scars become our golden badges of overcoming, and we can finally see ourselves as God's perfectly designed works of art. I plan to use this analogy and others throughout this book to help you visualize some of the process of putting the pieces of our lives back together again with Jesus' tender loving care.

---

[1] "Kintsugi" Wikipedia: Kintsugi ("golden joinery"), also known as kintsukuroi ("golden repair"), is the Japanese art of repairing broken pottery by mending the areas of breakage with lacquer dusted or mixed with powdered gold, silver, or platinum, a method similar to the maki-e technique. As a philosophy, it treats breakage and repair as part of the history of an object, rather than something to disguise. Retrieved from: en.wikipedia.org/wiki/Kintsugi#; Accessed 27 November 2020.

As I mentioned in the first paragraph of this book, the process can also be likened to following a road map or floor plan to find your way from one location to another. It can help us find our way from one place in our lives to another, and amazingly we get to choose the path we want to take. We can select the shortest, quickest, or most scenic routes. We can choose to get there as fast as possible or as slowly as we wish. You are the driver in the vehicle of your own life. You may have sustained some bumps, bruises, or even crashes along the way, but we have the incredible ability, with God's help to be fully restored and made even more beautiful than we were before our lives took a wrong turn. We can get back on track, and we can finish the race strong. So don't believe anyone who has told you that you can't get there from here, yes you can!

So the question then becomes, "Where are you going?" What is the easiest path to get there? Why do you want to go there? Who do you want to be when you get there? What do you hope to do when you get there? Who's in the driver's seat? Who's in the passenger seat? Who's in the backseat? Are you buckled in? Have you packed for the trip? How long will it take? How will you know when you've arrived? Will there be any stops along the way? Who's bright idea was this anyway? Are you ready?

As you can see, the questions are endless, and I could go on with them for the rest of this chapter, or we can just start answering some of them and see where it takes us. I vote for the second option. If you're with me, then let's start with "Where do you want to go or be?" Most of us have to answer that questions a hundred times a day. I have to go to the bathroom. I have to go to work or school. I have to go to the grocery store. I have to go to the mall. I have to go to the doctor's office; I have to, I have to, I have to. However, none of those actually answers the question, "Where do you *want* to go?" I'm guessing that contains an immeasurably different list of answers, or it may jog a whole new list of questions. Depending on your age, you may have been asking yourself this question very recently, or maybe you haven't asked yourself that question in many, many years. Some of you may have had that answer handed to you or forced upon you. Maybe your life took a dramatic turn somewhere along the line, and you have strayed far from where you intended to go or be. Some of you, like me, may have had your life come to a screeching halt because the road you were on came to a dead end.

Regardless of your situation, you can make a U-turn now or choose the road less traveled, speed up or slow down, but no matter where you are, just don't spin your wheels because there is an extraordinary life just waiting for you to step into it. However, for some of you, this may prove to be an extremely daunting or overwhelming question. Trying to determine the direction for your life may seem way too big a jump to make, given your current life situation. I want to remind you that you are the driver of your life no matter what other forces may be coming against you or prompting you to make a decision. What some of you may never have done in your life is to ask God where He thinks you should go or where He has opened the way for you to go.

Most people will ask their family or friends their opinion on such questions to help them ascertain which option makes the most sense or offers the most opportunities for success. So why not ask your new best friend Jesus His opinion too? Your immediate response may be because you have never heard Him speak to you before or that you can't hear Him. But what you may have never noticed is that God is talking to us all the time. God speaks to us in a myriad of ways every day. He may not speak in a Cecil B. DeMille[2] booming audible voice, but He is speaking. Ever notice when you keep seeing the same number sequence over and over? Ever notice when the same image keeps showing up everywhere you look? Ever notice when people all keep saying the same thing to you? Well, that's God talking to you through multiple means to try and get or direct your attention. As I mentioned previously, God has plans for each of us and our futures. "'For I know the plans I have for you,'" declares the LORD, 'plans to prosper you and not to harm you, plans to give you hope and a future'" (Jeremiah 29:11 NIV). The process is incredibly simple. You simply say, "Jesus will you show or tell me what plans You have for me?" That's it! One sentence, and you're there. Then what?

Then you listen. Some of you may actually hear Jesus speak something to you in your thoughts, or some specific thoughts may just pop into your head. Some of you may not hear

[2] "Cecil Blount DeMille" (August 12, 1881 – January 21, 1959) was an American film director and producer. Between 1914 and 1958, he made 70 features, both silent and sound films. He is acknowledged as a founding father of the American cinema and the most commercially successful producer-director in film history. His films were distinguished by their epic scale and by his cinematic showmanship. Retrieved from https://en.wikipedia.org/wiki/Cecil_B._DeMille; Accessed 11 January 2021.

anything but have a strong sense about something specific. Some of you may have a cinematic dream where you see yourself in this amazing new job. Some of you may suddenly notice a billboard on your way to work that you never noticed before that seems to just jump out at you or even seems to scream its message to you. Some of you may have the same conversation with multiple people where each of them repeats the same solution to you. That's God answering your question. The best reason to ask Jesus His opinion is that He knows the perfect solution for every single portion of your life and has already mapped out a perfect route for you. He knows what will make you happy right down into your bones. He knows the things you like and the things you detest. He knows what makes your heart sing and what will send you running for cover. He knows what scares you and what entices the very best out of you. He knows your talents and your shortcomings. He knows your potential, and He knows the very best path to achieve every ounce of that potential. So I recommend you just throw that question to Him and see what comes back.

Here's the part that I always marvel at—Jesus knows how big a step we can make at any time in our lives. He knows what we need to keep going forward. He knows what support, training or resources we're going to need. He knows where all the potholes and detours are located. He knows what fears we have and what wounds we may need healed before we can even take that first step. He knows it all. He knows us all. He knows every single part of who you are, where you've been, and what you need. Whether you know it or not, Jesus has been with you every step of the way, and I guarantee that no matter what your life may look like, His plans were always to prosper you and bless you. His love knows no bounds, and He will continue to walk with you every step of the way forward. The question for you is this: "Will you take His hand?"

Surely I Tell You

So let me share my experience with you when I first had to decide if I was actually going to take Jesus' hand and trust Him to lead my life. You will recall when I last spoke to Jesus, or rather He spoke to me, I was left sobbing on the floor in a puddle of tears when I realized it was God speaking to me about the plans He had for my life. Amazing, incredible, and quite frankly pretty unbelievable plans for my life. Among the many phenomenal things Jesus told me that glorious morning, He said that He had a house that He had picked out for me. A house that would be on a beautiful street; that would have Palladian windows across the whole back of the house; and that I would know that it was the house He had picked for me because I would find feathers there. Interesting, to say the least. Being an interior designer, I knew that Palladian windows referred to the Italian architect Andrea Palladio[3] known for his tall arched windows and porticos, but the feathers left me wondering just where in the world this house was going to be?

---

[3] "Andrea Palladio" (30 November 1508 – 19 August 1580) was an Italian Renaissance architect active in the Venetian Republic. Palladio, influenced by Roman and Greek architecture, primarily Vitruvius, is widely considered to be one of the most influential individuals in the history of architecture. Retrieved from: https://en.wikipedia.org/wiki/Andrea_Palladio. Accessed on 11 January 2021.

You will also recall that I had moved out of my home just prior to my husband's death, and due to the extreme trauma of that day, I had not been able to return there since that dreadfully fateful day. I welcomed the thought that God was going to move me away from the horror that home now held for me. Once I returned from my short time-out with my daughter and both of us were able to put one foot in front of the other again, I contacted a friend who was a real estate agent and asked her to show me any homes for sale in my region that had Palladian windows listed as a feature of the home. There were just three such options available.

The first home was located on a street resembling Lombard Street[4] in San Francisco, zig-zagging back and forth in sharp hairpin turns. It was not at all a beautiful street, in my opinion. The second home dead-ended at a cemetery, and I was absolutely sure that was not the ideal home for me. The third home, however, surprised me. It was clear on the opposite side of town and somewhat out in the country. As we turned onto the street, having momentarily forgotten the three prerequisites, I said, "Wow, this is such a beautiful street!" No sooner had the words come out of my mouth that I remembered and reiterated the first prerequisite: It would be on a "beautiful" street. My heart started to jump around in my chest. My mind began racing and wondering if this could actually be the house Jesus had told me about? In all honesty, I still was not entirely sure if I had simply imagined that entire godly encounter.

---

[4] "Lombard Street" is known for the one-way block on Russian Hill between Hyde and Leavenworth Streets, where eight sharp turns are said to make it the most crooked street in the world. Retrieved from: https://en.wikipedia. org/wiki/Lombard_Street_(San_Francisco). Accessed 11 January 2021.

Pulling up to the home, I noticed immediately that the front window was indeed a Palladian window; however, I also remembered equally quickly that Jesus had said the back of the home had Palladian windows, so this wasn't the confirmation I needed yet, but it certainly was a good start. The home was very lovely and quite appealing to me. It was more of an English Tudor-style than one of Italian renaissance architecture, and it was nicely framed by a backdrop of stately tall trees. The other homes on this street were equivalently regal, but my attention was sharply focused on this house. Was this indeed the one?

I waited impatiently as the real estate agent fumbled with the key lock box on the front door. It was not cooperating for the agent and was allowing time for my blood pressure to escalate in anticipation. Finally, the agent retrieved the front door key and opened the door. As it swung wide open, I could see the entire back of the house had the most majestic floor-to-ceiling Palladian windows I had ever personally seen. Tears literally burst out of my eyes as I saw these fabulously large windows. I sobbed in what I'm sure were completely unintelligible words, "This is my house. This is my house! He told me there were going to be Palladian windows!" The agent being a friend, was aware of my recent loss and clearly attributed this outburst to my overwhelming, grieving, fragile state. She tried to calm me and assure me that everything was going to be all right. I heard none of it as my heartbeat

"This is my house. This is my house! He told me there were going to be Palladian windows!"

was so loud in my own ears that it blocked anything coming in from the outside.

The agent stepped into the house and motioned for me to come along in as well. The front entrance was actually two steps up from the ground level, so I took the first step up with my eyes still wildly scanning and fixated on those massive Palladian windows. As I took that first step up, something crunched under my foot. I immediately stepped back down to look at what I had stepped on. There on the step were three feathers! Feathers! I nearly passed out when I saw them. I picked them up and sobbed uncontrollably. I kept saying the same thing over and over through a raging torrent of tears, "He told me, He told me, He told me." The poor agent didn't know what to say or do since I was clearly having a total meltdown. She said, "Just come in; it's okay, let me turn on some lights." I stood there in the entrance like I was petrified. I couldn't believe everything that was flooding my mind. "Beautiful street, Palladian windows, feathers, they were all there just like He said they would be." Once again, I knew I had heard God. I heard Him speak. God had actually spoken to me. More accurately, Jesus had spoken to me. And there, right in front of me, was actual tangible proof!

How was this all possible? My mind may have tried to trick me, but my eyes were beholding a real house—a real house! A really, really big house! I suddenly realized that this was a huge mansion of a house. A house that millionaire people live in. My eyes started scanning around to the towering columns, stunning wood flooring, soaring ceilings, sparkling chandeliers, shiny granite countertops, and I was brought back to my senses. This house was magnificent, but how much did it actually cost? In all my mind-bending excitement, I had never looked to see what the price was on any of these houses. This had to be a million-dollar house! I spoke out loud to God. "How in the world would I ever afford this kind of house?" And much to my continuing amazement, God spoke right back. "Surely I tell you, you will live in this house within two weeks' time." If my mind hadn't been blown before, it melted down then. "How God, how is that possible?" I was oblivious to whether I was talking out loud anymore or not. The agent was still busy turning on lights throughout this nearly five thousand square foot mansion of a house.

Even if I could afford this house, I couldn't even get a mortgage in two weeks' time. God continued, "Surely I tell you that tomorrow a woman will call and ask to rent your farmhouse, and you will know that I sent her because she will have third-level dressage horses." What? I was back to thinking I was losing my mind altogether now except for the chilling thought that I didn't even have my house on the market yet and, somehow, some lady was going to want to rent it. How was any of this possible, and what in the world was I doing in this mansion? Finally, the agent returned and eagerly started showing me around this gorgeous home. Everything was pristine because it had never been lived in yet. I was in awe of how beautifully everything was crafted. It was breathtakingly beautiful. Massively huge rooms and palatial views from the Palladian windows graced the back of every room of the house.

Floor-to-ceiling views left me dumbfounded as I walked believingly and then disbelievingly from room to room.

When at last I had finally seen all of this incredible house, I got up the nerve to ask the agent how much this house was listed for, and I was somewhat surprised at the actual price. The agent then showed me the multi-listing page. It had been on the market for two years because the housing market had crashed in 2008, and no one was buying such extravagant houses. The home had been built as a sample home in the area the builder was developing. The house had indeed been on the market for just under a million dollars! Now I was wondering if God was losing His mind. The agent informed me that the original builder had actually gone bankrupt, and the current developer was trying to recoup some of the losses by selling off this house. She encouraged me to make a low-ball offer and just see what happens. So in my mind-numbed state, I made an offer for half the original price, totally ignoring the fact that I still didn't even have my farmhouse on the market. I'd like to tell you that I actually had faith in God that day, but truthfully, I had now only heard God two times, and I wasn't yet completely sold, but rather, I was clearly operating out of a love-crazed mindset.

However, what happened the next day blew the top off of any doubt that I still had lingering that that still small voice was actually God. My sweet friend and real estate agent called me the following day and said that she had a question she wanted to ask me. She wondered if I would consider renting my farmhouse in light of the fact that I was now pursuing purchasing the mansion house? She said that she had received a call from a client that had been planning to rent another home but that it had been totally devastated by a drunken student rampage, and now they were at a total loss for what to do. The agent went on to tell me that the wife of the couple looking to rent was ecstatic to hear that a farm might be available to rent because she had third-level dressage horses![5] The agent said since I had show horses, she thought I would know what that actually meant. I'm pretty sure I dropped the phone at that point.

I knew what that meant because I showed horses in dressage and understood that they were highly trained and very valuable horses. That, however, was not what was holding my attention. Absolutely, inescapably, I was faced with the exact words and situation God had told me would happen. How was this all possible? My mind could not reckon with the reality I was facing. This new God interaction was utterly inconceivable, preposterous, beyond improbable, and completely real! Once again, everything that I had known about God up to that point was shattered with this realization. But God wasn't done fascinating me yet. The agent timidly continued. She said, "There is one catch, though; they need to be in the farmhouse within two weeks' time!" Apparently, the clients were both professors at the college, and their classes began in two weeks.

[5] "Dressage" Dressage a French term, most commonly translated to mean "training" is a competitive equestrian sport, defined by the International Equestrian Federation as "the highest expression of horse training" where "horse and rider are expected to perform from memory a series of predetermined movements." International Equestrian Federation competitions are held at all levels from amateur to the World Equestrian Games. Retrieved from: https://en.wikiquote.org/wiki/Dressage. Accessed 15 June 2021.

"Surely I tell you that in two weeks' time, you will live in this house," echoed through my mind like a freight train.

This was just all too impossible and yet it was actually happening. I asked the agent what I was supposed to do since I didn't even have an answer from the builder yet on the house, not that I could have actually arranged a settlement in two weeks anyway. She said she would press the builder for a quick response and get back to me. Well, if you haven't yet guessed it, the builder accepted my offer that day! No dickering, no counter-offer, no stipulations! And to even sweeten the pot more, they would allow me to rent the mansion until we could arrange the settlement. I could have immediate possession. But this story isn't done yet! God still wasn't done proving beyond a shadow of a doubt that He was not only talking, but He was in complete control of everything.

To say my faith had now skyrocketed would be a gross understatement. I was starting to believe that nothing was impossible, but I still had to traverse the mountain of packing up my whole house and moving everything that I owned into a brand new house. I quickly opted for my agent's suggestion to just hire a moving company to pack everything up and move it all for me. Good call, but I still actually had to make the call to the movers and get that whole ball rolling. Two weeks' time is not the normally suggested time allowance for such a huge moving endeavor, but I was feeling pretty invincible now. So I placed the call to the

I was starting to believe that nothing was impossible ...

only mover in town and asked if they could move me within the two-week allotment.

The moving company man did not exactly respond the way I had hoped. Instead of saying yes or I'll check the schedule, he instead chastised me. He said, "Lady, shame on you. If you're a local, then you ought to know that this is move-in week at the university. I don't have anything available. All my trucks and crews are booked." And in that very same moment, that still small voice inside me said, "Ask him again." *Huh?* So in blind obedience and complete desperation, I asked the not-so-friendly man to check again. His response was no more pleasant. He said, "Lady, I do all the scheduling of the trucks and the crews, and I told you I don't have anything available." Now what? The gentle and ever-so-assuring voice inside me answered my questioning mind, "Ask him again." This time I'm sure I just plain out begged the man to look and see if he had any kind of trucks or crew that might be able to help me. The now very annoyed moving manager said in a totally sarcastic voice, "Okay, hold on, lady."

I held on. I held on for what seemed like an hour. Finally, the mover came back on the line. His tone was one of sheer amazement. He said, "Lady, I don't know how it happened. I don't know when it happened, but I have a truck and crew, and the only day they are available is the very day you asked for." My phone hit the floor again! That, my friends, was the day I stopped believing that it was impossible to hear from God and that, as a matter of fact, He was ready, willing, and fully able to accomplish every single thing He said. That day, I believed!

Spiritual EMJ

Looking back on that whole amazing process, I see just how many times it took for me to believe that I was actually hearing from God. It may take you a few times, or it may take you a multitude of times. I am reminded of the Bible verse "…I believe; help my unbelief!" (Mark 9:24 ESV). In my heart, I believed it was God speaking, but my mind fought with that even being possible. I'm here to tell you it is undeniably and reliably true! God has, is, and will continue to speak to us. He is concerned with every part of our lives and wants to help us navigate the highways and byways of our life safely to achieve the fantastic destiny He has planned for us. The choice is entirely up to us. The true desires of our hearts were placed there by God when He knit us together in our mother's womb, and He wants us to fulfill those desires in the utmost possible manner.

What I didn't realize back then was God was also teaching me about faith. In the natural world, we hear "Seeing is believing," and for most of us, that is absolutely true. But with God, it is reversed. "Now faith is the substance of things hoped for, the evidence of things not seen" (Hebrews 11:1 KJV). We live in a natural, visible world, but God lives in a spiritual, unseen world. God was helping me to understand that I am both a natural being and a spiritual being. "For you created my inmost being; you knit me together in my mother's womb" (Psalm 139:13 NIV). Our "inmost being" is spiritual, and that is how it is possible for us to connect with God. Another Bible version of this same verse reads, "For You have possessed my reins, You cover me in my mother's belly" (LSV). In the natural "possessed my reins" refers to a person who would be holding the reins to a horse and directing the path it should take. God wants to help direct our path through our whole life. From the very moment He breathed life into us until we take our very last breath, He is with us.

I tell you all of that not to suddenly go all religious on you but to affirm that God is for us, not against us, and even when we can't believe our very own eyes, He's still holding onto us and protecting us no matter how long it takes us to believe it. He loves us in spite of ourselves. He knows the paths we are on, and He guides us, teaches us, and loves us even when we can't see, hear, understand or believe what He is saying. Better still, He wants to show us the amazing things we can hardly believe. He wants to show us glimpses of the marvelous things He planned for us from the very beginning of time. Astonishing things that blow our minds. Fabulous things that defy our imagination. Fantastic things that bring us joy, delight, and excitement for what comes next. He wants the child in us to come alive in excited anticipation. He wants to release us from all the things the world has piled on our backs and let us indulge in the impossible. That's the outrageous God I met that gorgeous morning ten years ago. The God that defies our physical minds and sets our spirits free to run headlong into His waiting arms to be loved beyond any comprehension we have previously held.

In the first days and weeks after my husband had passed away, I can assure you that I wasn't running headlong into anything but a brick wall. I had no idea where to start sweeping up all the mess. I didn't know what end was up or in what direction to turn. Everything was overwhelming. I knew that I had to pick up all the shattered pieces of my life and somehow figure out how to start to put them back together again. At first, well-intentioned family and friends would tell me to take one day at a time, but some days, I actually couldn't seem to go from one minute to the next. So fairly quickly, I sought the help of my pastor, my doctor, and a therapist. I didn't realize it at the time, but that was exactly what I needed to do. I needed help for my exhausted body, my traumatized spirit, and my bewildered mind, and that is exactly the plan I advocate for in this book. Seek help for your whole self. Whether you know it now or not, you are actually made up of three parts. You have a physical body, a soul, and a spirit. All three need to be addressed if you are to successfully resolve the issues or crashes that arise in your life.

When your life is a train wreck, you have to start slowly. Be tender with yourself. Don't hesitate to ask for help because it really is easier to deal with the mess when you have some assistance. I quickly found that when I picked up one piece, another one would fall back down. I kept picking up pieces and dropping others. It only added to the frustration and crippling weariness. Let me assure you that it is not a sin to ask for help. It's not a sign that you are weak or incompetent or inept. You simply

> **When your life is a train wreck, you have to start slowly. Be tender with yourself**

need some reinforcements. Family and friends are not always equipped to help; although they may be very vocal in their advice, it's usually wise to seek well-qualified professionals for each aspect of your self—spirit, soul, and body.

Let me employ another simile to illustrate the process. Since a train wreck is really messy, let's just go with a car crash. You are driving along, and suddenly you collide with another vehicle. Your airbag goes off, and you are momentarily stunned and disoriented with the situation. When the bag deflates, your mind starts racing to assess the current state of affairs. Your mind does a supersonic review of all your body parts, all your car parts, and all the surrounding wreckage. You make a Herculean effort to figure out what just actually happened and what you're going to do now. *Am I bleeding, breathing, is anything broken? Who hit me, or who did I hit? Is anybody else hurt? Oh gosh, there's glass all over the place because some of the windows are shattered and broken into tiny pieces everywhere.* Your mind is on overload and is randomly firing questions by the thousands without waiting for the answers.

Life can be pretty much the same when something you least expected suddenly happens, and you are caught in the maelstrom of the situation or crisis. First, your mind goes numb for a while, and you're stunned. Then your mind tries valiantly to battle through the torrential rain of questions pouring into your head. *What just happened? Who hit me? Am I okay? Now, what am I going to do?* Depending on the severity of your life situation, the questions will continue pouring in by the thousands. Strangely the answers seem to swirl somewhere out in space, very much out of your reach. You grapple with innumerable possible solutions to the whirl of questions bombarding your mind until you just want to pass out in debilitating weariness. But when you boil it all down, it comes to one simple question, "Now what?"

This is exactly the situation I found myself in ten years ago, and I knew immediately I wasn't going to be able to do this alone. I needed help, and I needed it right away. I needed a situational EMT.[6] Just like the car crash victim, I needed the ambulance EMT to come in and evaluate the overall situation and what needed to be done, and in what order in my worldly crash. Likewise, God is a God of order and our spiritual EMT. He knows what needs to be done regarding our spirit and soul as well. All of our being needs to be evaluated and a plan of action determined. So we are literally back at the "YOU ARE HERE" sign, and we're surveying all the possible routes, but now we know that the best path forward must include not only our body but our spirit and soul too.

So let's start to break down the evaluation process of our life crash. We need to know just what needs the most immediate attention. What are the priorities that must be attended to first that will ensure your safety, your health, your sanity, your family, your finances, and the remaining list of life concerns for

---

[6] "An emergency medical technician" (EMT), also known as an ambulance technician, is a health professional that provides emergency medical services. [1][2] EMTs are most commonly found working in ambulances. In English-speaking countries, paramedics are a separate profession that has additional educational requirements, qualifications, and scope of practice. Retrieved from: https://en.wikipedia.org/wiki/Emergency_medical_technician. Accessed 13 January 2021.

your overall well-being before we can start putting one foot in front of the other?

When it comes to first aid, there are three Ps to remember—**p**reserve life, **p**revent deterioration, and **p**romote recovery.[7] Without exception, the first priority is ensuring your safety and your life. In my humble opinion, God created doctors for a reason; to help our bodies to function well and help us in emergencies. Seeking medical advice and appropriate medication for both physical and mental issues is prudent. You can't put one foot in front of the other if you can't stand up or think. Be kind to your body. Get the medical attention you need and seek counseling to save your day-to-day sanity. Self-care is extremely important when you are dealing with the really rough spots in your life.

If you are in a physically abusive, domestically violent, or dangerous personal situation, extreme caution is of paramount importance. There are resources available to help you navigate a plan to safely exit your situation. Safety must come first for you, your children, and any others that are at risk. While 911 is the first option if you are in immediate danger, there are other national numbers for assistance as well. Two such numbers are National Domestic Violence Hotline: 1-800-799-7233 and National Suicide Prevention Lifeline: 1-800-273-TALK (8255). These call personnel are trained to help you and fully understand the severity of the situation you may be in. They

---

[7] "Three P's of First Aid" Idaho Medical Academy; Three C's of an Emergency & Three P's of First Aid; Retrieved from: https://www.idahomedicalacademy. com/the-three-cs-of-an-emergency-and-the-three-ps-of-first-aid/. Accessed 13 January 2021.

can and will help direct you and guide you to safety as well as advise you of locally available resources for you. Your safe welfare is their prime concern.

Preventing deterioration in an accident involves keeping the person from panicking, going into shock, stroke, arrhythmia, hypothermia, or any number of secondary stages of health crises. In a personal crisis, you need to ascertain if your life needs a band-aid or surgery. You need to stop the bleeding, which ultimately involves a change of direction from where you have been going up to this point. Often we get a wake-up call in our lives as a warning that we need to address the problem before we are in crisis mode. Heed those warnings and seek help early. If you address the problem early, it's guaranteed to be easier sooner rather than later. Warning signs are just that, danger ahead. Stop—turn around!

Preventing spiritual deterioration is equally important and should not be ignored. However, many people don't even know what the warning signs are to avoid them. Fear, anxiety, depression, distress, dread, and anger are just a few and can easily lead to dozens and dozens of more extenuating conditions. Getting to the root causes of these drivers is essential to averting much more disabling circumstances. Figuring out who or what is driving these feelings is absolutely essential if you are going to mitigate them. The tough part is that, unlike bleeding, you can't actually see these warning signs with your eyes, but they show up as feelings or emotions. So determining the healing process has to be an internal one of assessing the damage. Where are the emotional wounds, and how do we bandage or treat them? Regrettably, many people will self-medicate on the outside, trying to treat what hurts on the inside. It's not at all uncommon that actually looking at what is broken on the inside is far scarier than seeing what is broken on the outside. But the truth is that what is broken on the outside is really just a consequence of what is broken on the inside. Treating those aches and pains takes a different kind of EMT and doctor.

Promoting recovery is just one of the aims of this book. I desire to help you to assess the damage in both your outside physical world and your internal spiritual world. Helping you to face what is real and right in front of your face, as well as looking at the raw and sometimes gory internal realms of your life. But with a different end game goal, one of complete healing and not just bandaging the damage, so you can live in the fullness and happiness you were created for in the first place. That place really does exist, and we're heading there now. Come in; the doctor is waiting.

As with any doctor's visit, the doctor is going to ask you why you are there. What is your problem or problems? Oddly, you are actually hoping he is going to tell you what your problem is. So the impasse is in going from the symptoms to the cause to figure out what the best plan of treatment will be. Of course, for our physical doctor, the goal is getting you to feel better, but our heavenly Physician ultimately wants to get you completely healed. While the worldly doctor will assess your bodily functions, he likely will not attempt to determine your spiritual ailments whatsoever, thereby providing you with only one-third of the necessary treatment plan for your total wellness. Fortunately, God is happy to provide the other two-thirds of your evaluation to complete your full healing and restoration.

Depending on your condition, you will seek the most likely type of specialist to help you with your problem. There is no end to the types of doctors from which you can seek help. There are surgeons, general practitioners, psychiatrists, heart specialists, pediatricians, dietitians, opticians, and the list goes on and on. The danger is that as specialists, they are trained to look for very specific symptoms, and possible causes yet can easily overlook very pertinent factors outside their specialization. Their assessment will be based on what they are trained to look for. If your problem doesn't seem to fall into any of their characteristic symptoms, they may tell you that you are fine. They see no problem, that is, within their scope, purview, or specialty. Thank goodness for second opinions. I encourage you to seek Christian counselors, ministers, pastors, and deliverance ministries (just to name a few) that can help tap into the Holy Spirit to address your spiritual concerns too.

You Find What You Are Looking For

The truth of the matter may be that your physical problem actually has a spiritual cause or driver. Many physical pains are a result of the pain from a wounding to your soul, which encompasses your mind, will, and emotions. Literally, these woundings drive much of our perspective on life and happiness. Our life experiences determine how we see the world. Yet, there is a choice. We can decide how we want to see the world and what we want to focus on. The perspective we look from determines what we see. So let's go back to our car crash analogy for a few minutes to gain a better understanding of how our view colors our perspective. This time though, we are going to look at things from the outside of the car. The car accident has already happened, and the vehicles are resting askew in the intersection. Several people have witnessed the accident and are running to the scene. I'm going to take a bit of stereotypical license here to make the comparisons, so please don't take it personally if you happen to fall into any of these title roles. This is a hypothetical example, and no character assassinations are intended.

The first person to reach the car is a lawyer. His response is, "Are you okay? I saw the whole thing. I'm happy to represent you if this goes to court. I can get you out of this mess. I know the law and all your legal rights." The second person to reach the car is an insurance agent. She says, "Are you okay? I saw the whole thing. I hope you have insurance to cover all of this. Do you have insurance?" The third person on the scene is a pastor. He assures you that he has already called 911, and the ambulance is on the way. "Now, let me say a prayer for you till they get here." The fourth person hurrying up to the car is out of breath from running up the street. She was walking her new dog, and he had broken free from her and ran right into the path of the other car in the accident. She is so relieved that the other driver stopped so quickly and missed hitting her brand new puppy. She's really so sorry that it caused this accident, though. There is an elderly lady on the opposite corner that is crying and trying to explain to the other onlookers, "I saw the whole thing. It was awful. What a mess! Both cars are wrecked. I don't know how they could ever fix them again." Lastly, the guy in the car just behind the two crunched cars does a U-turn and leaves the scene. He doesn't have time to deal with this mess. He's got important things he needs to attend to today. He hopes he isn't going to be late for his meeting because of all this wasted time. Thankfully the police and ambulance arrive on the scene and start to attend to the accident victims and get the eyewitness reports.

The EMTs run to each vehicle and evaluate each driver. They know the three P's of first aid and quickly put all of their accident training into action—preserve life, prevent deterioration, and promote recovery. They start down the comprehensive list of emergency response evaluations. What condition is each driver in? What is the most critical infirmity? Are either of the drivers in a life-threatening condition? What precautions are necessary before proceeding with treatment? What is the best method of care until we can get them to the hospital? They continue evaluating the situation working diligently through their accident triage process, and taking all the necessary precautions while performing all the appropriate first aid. Meanwhile, the police are reviewing all the accident details.

Drivers' names, addresses, insurance, owner's registration, the vehicle makes and models, license numbers, accident location, vehicle conditions, eyewitness names and reports, traffic control, and tow truck request are all being attended to. The drivers are packed carefully into the ambulances and taken to the hospital for further medical attention, the vehicles are towed from the intersection, and all the shattered glass and debris are cleaned up from the scene of the accident. Order is restored. Job is done. Or is it? Well, as anyone who has ever been in an accident, you know that's not the end. The EMTs need to attend to the person until they get to the hospital; the drivers will get another round of questions, tests, X-rays, and evaluations. The police officers have to analyze all the eyewitness testimonies and then finally file a report of the accident. They will surely have to speak with the insurance companies and may eventually have to appear in court. The job's not over till it's over. At this point, we actually don't know what we don't know. There's still so much to process.

Let's make the comparison now to the multitude of perspectives and see how this all relates to how we process our own life situations. Interestingly, all the eyewitnesses who saw this accident had very different testimonies. How is that possible if they all saw the same accident? Each of them testified that they had seen the whole accident, so shouldn't their testimonies match; case closed? No! Why? Because each witness had a different view of the accident and was looking through their own life experience eyeglasses. Each eyewitness represents different personal viewpoints and different perspectives both in what they saw with their eyes as well as how they perceive the world. Each person is telling the truth, their truth, what they saw, but it doesn't make the other testimonies untrue or wrong; they are just from a different perspective. That's how all of life actually happens. We all have a certain viewpoint or vantage point for how we see and experience life.

Like the police officer, we have to determine what really happened and what are the subsequent consequences. We often fall into one of the characters in the accident scenario. Life is what happens to us when we're standing still, just walking by, or it's flying past us. We see everything in part. Some of it is good; some not so good. Sometimes we are taking a creative part in what is happening around us, and sometimes, life just plain happens to us. The part we can control, however, is how we look at things and how we react to them. Every day, a thousand things happen in our daily earthly lives that we see or partake in, and we get to decide if it will bring us joy or sorrow. Likewise, a thousand things happen in our daily spiritual lives that we don't see but impact our joy or sorrow. I'd like to give you a glimpse of what is happening in that spiritual realm as we put on our detective hats and scrutinize each of the eyewitness reports. Spy glasses ready? Here goes.

You are the driver of the second car, and you just rear-ended the car in front of you at the intersection when they stopped short after beginning to proceed through the intersection. You were already moving and saw the light turn green, and the preceding car began to turn left, clearing the lane for you to proceed through the intersection without having to reduce your speed. Regrettably, the preceding car suddenly stopped short, and you collided with their rear bumper. As you will recall, the lawyer was the first person to reach your vehicle, and he was ready, willing, and able to represent you if you needed to go to court. Lawyers, as you probably well know, are litigators of the law and love to delve into every possible detail of it when in court. They surely know every detail about "the law." In the spirit realm, the "lawyer or religious spirits" function through the folks who are happy to tell you about every sin or wrong thing they see or think you are doing; of course, in their humble opinion.

The second person to reach you was the insurance agent, and she was genuinely concerned that you have insurance to be sure that all the costs would be covered to repair your vehicle. This agent of concern is the person who wants to be sure that both you and they have "fire insurance" in the spiritual realm. Meaning they have accepted Christ just to ensure they won't be going to eternity in the fiery pit of hell. They prefer their spiritual water lukewarm, not too hot, thank you.

Trotting in third to your crunched vehicle is the pastor. Nice guy, kind, gentle, and very reassuring. He knows you are in good hands with Jesus, but he doesn't necessarily understand what all the fuss is about the supernatural. He's definitely a believer, and his prayers are contrite. He trusts that God is going to work all things for good. True, for sure.

Puffing and a bit out of breath, comes the gal whose puppy managed to slip his collar and sprint care-freely into traffic. Horrified, the girl regains control of her precious pup and apologizes for all the mayhem that he has caused. She's not old enough to drive, so she is totally oblivious to the full gamut of the chaos that has just happened. Seeing that no one seems terribly hurt and she knows nothing about reporting to the police officer, she reprimands her naughty puppy and goes on her merry way. In the spirit world, our young friend is a brand new believer, and she's just a babe in her newly found Christian faith. She's pretty much oblivious to everything in the spiritual world as well.

The elderly woman across the street is still explaining to all the onlookers just how awful the accident was even though she covered her eyes just before the impact. She knew what was coming and just couldn't bear to see it. She turned away from the screeching tires and crashing noise lest she be near the actual accident. She stopped in her tracks, covered up, and wagged her head in disbelief when she finally opened her eyes. Kids and dogs out of control, speeding motorists, this world is surely full of careless, unruly people. Life's experience has jaded this woman's view of the world. She has come to a standstill of disbelief, much like the Israelites of the Old Testament. Even the mere potential for disaster holds her fast in fear.

Our U-turn guy is nowhere in sight by now. He's long gone and onto something of real importance. He doesn't have time for stupid people who do stupid things. Besides, stupid people get what they deserve. There are consequences for driving around like an idiot. If they had half a brain in their heads, they'd be paying attention and not frittering away all their time on such dumb stuff. They need to keep their minds on the business at hand and not daydreaming away their lives. Right? Our U-turn man is self-righteous as well as self-centered. He's too busy to worry about other people's problems or suffering. His heart is hardened, and kindness seems like weakness to him. No doubt he avoids all things spiritually as well. Where's the productivity in all of that hogwash?

In our little traffic vignette, we've got two other participants that you may have forgotten about but are very significant in their roles. Our police officer is the one who must sift through all things reported. Only God truly sees the whole of our lives from His heavenly perspective. And there was the EMT who exemplifies the Holy Spirit, who is our helper. He comes in and gives us guidance and assistance with all our life's maladies.

Lastly, but certainly not the least, you may be asking, where was Jesus in all of this? Good question! He was in the passenger seat right next to you. He never leaves or abandons you. He is there in every part of our lives. He is our help in times of trouble, and He helps us overcome every circumstance, every problem, every heartache, every failure, every grief, every sorrow, every disappointment, and the list never ends. As I've already emphasized, He is the answer to everything.

> Jesus never leaves or abandons you. He is our help in times of trouble ... He is the answer to everything

The question then becomes, who are you in all of these characters? What life crashes have you experienced? What is your perspective? From what vantage point are you looking at life? What are you looking for? How do you see the world? What color glasses are you looking through? Who are you spiritually? Who is Jesus to you? Who is God to you? All good questions to ponder and decide. Because if you don't know who you are or where you are looking to go, it's impossible to get there. You will just keep crashing into things, and life will just be a series of accidents. But thankfully, there is hope for you. Yay!

Remember the EMTs? They are the ones who help. They help you assess where you are and what condition you are in. What is your most critical infirmity? Are you in a life-threatening situation? What precautions are necessary before proceeding with treatment? What is the best method of care until you get to a doctor? Your spiritual EMT is the Holy Spirit, and He is able to help you navigate all these questions and see the marvelous life journey God has prepared for you. The process is always two-sided: physical and spiritual. We all need help to manage our day-to-day life challenges, and we certainly need spiritual guidance to overcome the parts of our lives that are hidden deep within our hearts and souls. Working both together, you will come through the process much quicker and with greater ease. Help is only a prayer and phone call away.

Is the Bible a GPS?

What a silly question, or is it? How we view the Bible, religion, or life in general, can most definitely impact how we move towards or away from life's problems. Since I've already dated myself, I can tell you that when Global Positioning Systems (GPS) first emerged for public use, I was scared to death of them. I was very adept at reading maps and figuring out how to make my way from one place to another. I was never afraid to take long trips because I would have charted all of the route numbers that I needed to follow, and then I'd write the route numbers on an index card in magic marker, so it was easy to read while driving. Yes, index cards! And by the way, they still work! But my husband loved the newest technology gadgets and couldn't wait for me to try out this new-fangled directional tool.

On the first trip that I used my husband's Garmin[8] GPS, I was traveling to Long Island, New York, from central Pennsylvania. I had never been to this destination before, so I did my usual map charting, but my husband assured me I would not need any of that with the assistance of "Carmen." The nickname we gave the woman who voiced all the directions so aptly. Yes, that's right, her name was Carmen Garmin. We were so imaginative back then! So off I went to New York with my sister and daughter to a bridal shower for a friend. All went well until we discovered that Carmen had chosen a different route for us to travel, which involved going through the Holland Tunnel under the Hudson River, which connects you to lower Manhattan, New York, on the far side.

There is a slightly gargantuan problem that we discovered about our GPS system. It didn't work underground, and that it takes several minutes to reconnect with the satellite system once you resurface. That wouldn't necessarily be a big problem except that there are six lanes of vehicles moving at about 50

---

[8] "Garmin" Garmin Ltd. (shortened to Garmin, stylized as GARMIN, and formerly known as ProNav) is an American multinational technology company founded in 1989 by Gary Burrell and Min Kao in Lenexa, Kansas, United States, with headquarters in Olathe, Kansas. Since 2010, the company is incorporated in Schaffhausen, Switzerland. The company specializes in GPS technology for automotive, aviation, marine, outdoor, and sport activities. Retrieved from: https://en.wikipedia.org/wiki/Garmin. Accessed on 25 January 2021.

mph exiting the Holland Tunnel, and you have approximately 30 seconds to get into the correct lane to go either north or east before you find yourself smack-dab in the middle of the Manhattan shopping district. As luck would have it that particular day, New Yorkers were enjoying a street fair, and six lanes of traffic came to a long, sobering stop. Carmen apparently wanted to shop as she repeatedly redirected us around and around Manhattan in a fruitless circle. Finally, in utter frustration and desperation, I looked around and said to my copilot sister, "Shut Carmen up and open your window." No, we didn't throw her out, although the temptation to do so was great, but I told my confused sister, "Point to the other cars (all six lanes of them) that we want to cross lanes to the right." Without Carmen or my trusty maps, I resorted to my Girl Scout training and deduced that the sun rose in the east, and since we were heading east, we were going to head towards the sun.

I tell you all of that to give you the easiest and most effective GPS lesson you will ever need. When in trouble, when in doubt, when you're in a jam, head towards the sun! The "Son" of God that is, Jesus. He knows every path, and He knows exactly the right one to get you where you need to be. Jesus must have sent divine intervention that day because astoundingly, all six lanes of New Yorkers actually let us cross over and take the exit east! Now that's a miracle if ever there was one. I love New York! We found our way back on route and made it to the bridal shower a little worse for wear but just in time.

By now, you may be asking, "So what does this all have to do with the Bible?" Well, the Bible can act as a divine GPS system to offer the training and wisdom necessary to survive every one of life's wrong turns and get you back on track. The Bible not only has the capacity to map out countless ways to maneuver you out of the tight spots but also be a perfect travel director to plot the best course to avoid the jams that put your life in gridlock. It's loaded with stories and instruction, but even better, it is loaded with the love of God for everything you will face in this life and the next!

The Bible is loaded with guidance—stories and instructions to manuever you out of any tight spot. It is filled with the love of God to answer everything you will ever face in this life or the next!

Chapter 3

What's Your Truth?

Who's Got Your Leash?

I'm pretty sure I hear some of you clearing your throats and reminding me that I said I wasn't going to find my answers in religion and wondering why I'm saying that the Bible is going to manage to do all of that. I knew I had astute readers! So let me clarify myself a bit more. The Bible isn't a religion book. What! I'm pretty sure a few of you are now in absolute shock over that statement. Stay with me here. The Bible is not about a religion but about faith, hope, and love. Christianity is a faith in a God of mercy, love, and forgiveness. How you view God will directly affect the way you see the Bible, eternity, and life in general. It will determine if you see the Bible as an instruction manual, a bunch of interesting but confusing stories, a lot of to-do about nothing, or a love story.

Before I met God personally on that amazing summer morning, I absolutely saw the Bible as an instruction manual of how to stay out of hell in eternity. My faith was an insurance policy or a get-out-of-fiery-jail-free pass. The Bible literally scared the hell out of me! To me, the Bible stories represented a non-relational God who got really ticked off at the first two people He made and sent them to earth to do hard labor for a really long time. Then He got really frustrated with all their children and created a flood to wash them all off the face of the earth. Then the couple of people who actually listened to Him and got in that big boat survived until they started acting dumb, and the Egyptians made them build a bunch of pyramids. Then God cut them a break and let them go wander around in the desert for a really long time trying to find this promised land thing. And well, it was just one story after another about a really unhappy God who kept sending plagues and wiping people out.

I was taught a God of fear and punishment and kept wondering where the God "who so loved the world" was in all of that? How was any of that about love? How could any of that possibly be about love? Well, the answer is that it was my perspective. I only saw one side of the story. I only saw one side of God. I only saw what I was taught to see. My vision was narrowed to only a God of judgment instead of a God of mercy and grace. I only saw a God that was trying to "take us out" instead of one that was trying "to get us out." Those are vastly different intentions. The generation that taught me was stuck in the Old Testament part of the Bible and never made it into the New Testament. They nearly completely missed telling us about Jesus. Their intention was actually admirable. They were trying to keep us from eternal hellfire, but they spent so much time focusing on hell that they missed Jesus standing in heaven with the door wide open.

So our focus, our view, our perspective, our experience, our mindsets, our teachers, and everything about how we have lived impacts how we actually see things and how we live into them. I want to help you start looking through a different set of lenses than you may have been looking through up to this point in your life. Or at least broaden the viewfinder to help you adjust what you are seeing. Let's take the scales off from your eyes[1] and help you saddle up in front of a Drive-In sized view of who God really is.

Thus far in this book, I have been talking in similes but now I want to give you some practical ways to assess what's going on both inside and outside of you. And if you don't like either or both of them, how to take steps to change them. I also want to show you the God who has been reaching down into the world for thousands of years and pulling us out of the mess we've gotten ourselves into. He is real. He is loving, and He is for you, not against you. Nobody is going to run to a God they believe is going to throw them into the fire, so I want to show you a God who wants to hold you, comfort you, and love you beyond your wildest imagination.

I posed a question at the beginning of this chapter: "Who's got your leash?" That may sound a bit rude but be patient with me; I want to turn you loose. We are all held captive by something, but we seldom realize to what extent. I certainly didn't have any idea of how distorted my image of God was for

---

[1] Acts 9:18 NLT "Instantly something like scales fell from Saul's eyes, and he regained his sight. Then he got up and was baptized."

52 years! Imagine my surprise when this loving Jesus showed up on my hotel balcony. Like all of us, I just didn't know what I didn't know. God was supposed to be mean, scary, and show up with lots of thunder and lightning. It sounds silly when I write it out, but honestly, that was my image of God. I think it was why when He first spoke, He said the only things I could identify with. "Do not put the Lord your God to the test!" In other words, don't make me come down there and straighten you out! That was what God was supposed to sound like. That is what made sense in my concept of God, but it was so, so limited and so, so jaded and so, so not true.

So that leads us to some interesting questions then. Let me pose a couple to start with. What is your view of God? Oh, it just occurred to me that you may not even have or believe in God. Well, that's at least a starting place all the same. My sincere hope is that you continue to read anyway. You may learn some useful information in the process. Ultimately, I hope that my testimony and the information in this book will encourage you to keep seeking answers about God and Jesus. I firmly believe that if you've picked up this book that God has a divine appointment planned for you and a new freedom of spirit. If you do happen to believe in God, is He nice or not so nice? Is He an angry God? Is He a vengeful God? Is He alive in your life, or does He just live on the pages in some book called the Bible? Is He all-powerful and all-knowing? Is He real or just out there somewhere in the universe? Is He merciful and kind or not so much? Well, that's many questions already. My intent is for you to think about what you think about God. Who, what, where is He in your life, if at all? I encourage you to spend some time mulling over all of that in your mind. Selah! I always wanted to write that. It's a word in the Bible that means sit and think about that for a while. Write it out if that helps, or maybe you want to write some of your own questions about how you view God or ask God a few questions of your own. By the way, there are no wrong answers, so don't worry if you're getting any of this right. It's simply a place of departure in assessing where you are on your journey with God.

Unless you have had some kind of encounter with God, your view of God has probably come from someone else. It generally starts with our parents or teachers; in my case, it was mostly from the nuns who taught at my elementary school or the priests who had charge over our church. I lived in a small community, which was predominately Catholic. With little other influence, I had no reason to doubt what I was being taught. We were even taught to pray for those who did not attend our church or school so that they wouldn't go to hell. I still remember standing on the sidewalk in front of a house that I knew had a boy who didn't go to our school, thus was clearly not Catholic, and praying for him. I was genuinely worried for him and simply could not understand what in the world his parents could have been thinking not to send him to our school so he wouldn't go to hell.

You may not have learned about God for some time in your life. Or, if you are from a younger generation, you may actually have been blessed to know Jesus loves you. You may or may not have had good experiences around your faith. You may have been hurt by Christian people who are supposed to be kind but were a far stretch from that ideal. You may have parents that come from different religious faith backgrounds. That can certainly be confusing. You may have parents who don't happen to believe there is a God or that the universe is your god. All of which can make this exercise of thinking about who God is a bit more challenging. But you may be relieved to know I don't plan to debate any of these views. My point is to simply have you think about the influences that have occurred in your life up to this time that have shaped how you think about God.

Why is that important, you may ask? Because those are the thoughts and people who are likely holding your leash. And like the puppy who slipped his collar in our earlier scenario, you may want or need to be released from whatever or whoever may be holding you bound or holding you back from believing that God is unequivocally loving. This list may be extremely long or amazingly short. One person can impact your perception immensely, and that individual, in all probability, was not God. So who or what is speaking into your life? What is their viewpoint on God, and why? How are they influencing what you think or believe, and does that match your own experience? Are they positive or negative viewpoints?

As we have already ascertained, our life experiences will color our view of who God is. Our thoughts, feelings, and emotions will also play a major role in our perceptions. If you have been wounded by someone emotionally, there's hurt there, and it can create all kinds of feelings and false thinking about love overall. There are massive volumes of explanations on why bad things happen to good people, and they are helpful when you are dealing with the really difficult or traumatic stuff of life, but they don't change the fact of who God is or His character. God is love, plain and simple. I didn't always believe that myself, so I don't actually expect that you may just take my word for it either. Indeed I may not be able to explain every situation

God is love, plain and simple

you may have found yourself in, but I can tell you what I have learned through my experiences, and you can weigh that against what you are currently believing or struggling to understand.

Very few people, if any, make it through life unscathed by some emotional pain, suffering, betrayal, abuse, accident, bad decision, lies, hurt, spite; you name it. Somewhere along the way, life dealt you a bad hand. Something went wrong, perhaps even dreadfully wrong, and we are left to figure out how it happened and what we're going to do about it. As we have already determined there are countless perspectives, opinions, and viewpoints on what you need to do and how you should do it. These well-meaning folks are speaking from both their life and emotional experiences but are they speaking from love? If they have been left at the altar, I can pretty much guarantee you they are not speaking from a loving viewpoint. Understandably, if they have been lied to, cheated on, or heartbroken, they are not looking through a clear lens of love. So, if we have all been affected by some hurtful life experience somewhere along our lives, how do we find an unbiased view of love? Yup, you guessed right, Jesus. Told you He has the answer to every problem.

Jesus is the manifest example of God that we could actually see, hear, and feel right here on earth. He exemplified the perfect character of God for us to know unmistakably who God was, is, and always will be. Jesus exemplified what true love looks like for us. Of course, this brings us full circle to whether you actually believe in a God at all. If you don't believe in God, my hope is that you will be closer to believing in God by the end of this book and accepting who Jesus really is for you. In the meantime, let's keep digging into what your truth looks like.

What's Your Truth?

Let's check out what kind of glasses you are wearing: sunglasses, bifocals, magnifiers, designer rose-colored glasses, or maybe you've gotten your binoculars out to look this situation over from a safe distance. Interestingly, they all represent how you normally prefer to look at things in your life. Some of you want an in-depth analysis; some would rather see both sides of the coin, some would prefer a bit of a toned-down view, some just want the facts, some would prefer just the sunny side of things, and some of you would like the ten-foot-pole distance, thank you very much. Regardless of how close or far you want to check things out, in the final analysis, you will realize that it all always boils down to the same thing—love.

We all desire to be loved, we all need love or at least acceptance, and we all need to feel lovable. Nothing wrong with that. How can I be so sure about that definitive statement? Easy, believe it now or not, we are all made in God's image, and God is love. It's just as simple as that. We were created by love, for love, and to give love. That's a lot of love, and I'm here to testify that God has more love for you than your heart could possibly hold.

Not only have I personally felt this love for myself, but I have felt God's unbridled, unlimited, immeasurable, immense love poured out for many, many others too. His love truly knows no bounds.

But I digress, back to figuring out what may have you tied up in knots. Like me, you may have come from a dysfunctional family; you may have suffered verbal, physical, or sexual abuse, abandonment, an alcoholic or drug-addicted parent, or a betrayal by a friend or family member. You may have had been the brunt of bullying, mocking, or taunting. You may have been the middle child that never measured up regardless of who you were compared to. Maybe you had very busy or successful parents that never had the time for you or were constantly pushing you to be something more or something else. Maybe you were born into a family from the wrong side of the tracks. No matter what your circumstances may have been or still are, life's maladies and challenges are endless, and no one is exempt; rich or poor, weak or strong, short or tall, we all have things to overcome. All those experiences shape who we have become but not necessarily who we are. As I've said before, what has happened to you does not define who you really are or who you were designed to be.

As a matter of fact, every day we have hundreds of choices we get to make and how we are going to respond to the world around us. We have the option to do any number of responses. We can get mad or even. We can listen or shout. We can accept or deny. We can be happy or sad. We can change the world, or we can sit and watch it go by. We can challenge the status quo, or we can go with the flow. We can embrace change or hang tightly onto what is safe and secure. We can trust or fear. We can forgive or hold a grudge. We can sing and dance, or we can stomp and pout. Somedays I feel like I do all of these things, and generating all those decisions can be altogether exhausting. However, you may feel that your decisions are being controlled and fashioned by someone else and that your choices have already been shaped for you, and you have to fight to have any control of your life. Some of you may feel that the universe is in control of it all, and your fate has already been sealed.

The truth is we do have free will, but there are millions of people and circumstances that impact our choices and our beliefs. You may have heard it said that you are what you eat, and metaphorically, I guess that may be true. What exactly are you feeding yourself? Not just your body but also your spirit and soul because all three will most definitely impact how you are feeling both inside and out. Sweets, caffeine, drugs, alcohol, medicine, preservatives, red dye number five will all contribute to how your physical body is feeling. Anger, bitterness, hatred, anxiety, fear, tension, frustration, angst, and distrust are sure to keep your soul in a rotten mood. Suspicion, unforgiveness, judgment, hard-heartedness, manipulation, untrustworthiness, impatience, and hopelessness will crush your spirit in a hurry. Conversely, fruits, vegetables, water, and all things organic will blissfully surprise your body. Peace, understanding, mercy, grace, trust, confidence will go a long way to calming the bad feelings raging in your soul. Tenderness, joy, patience, love, forgiveness, gentleness, and zeal will most definitely make your spirit soar. No doubt about it, that's a lot of decision-making for any given day, and it doesn't take much imagination to determine a steady diet of the nasty food, emotions, and feelings is going to make you sick and miserable. While feasting on a healthy, peaceful, and loving diet will successfully fill your spirit, soul, and body with joy and gladness. Your choice really does control how you are going to look, feel, and function in your world.

Since I'm obviously having a field day juxtaposing all these choices, let me flip the question around and ask you what's eating you? Who is stealing your peace? Who is poisoning your attitude? Who is sullying your mindset? Why are you making the choices that even you don't like? Is anyone forcing your hand? Both your answers and your perspective will influence the decisions you make and how you see yourself, the world, and God. I've taken you through this whole exercise to show you that you need to know the ending before the beginning. You need to know where you want to end up, what is holding you back, blocking your path, or tainting your vision before you even begin.

From Omega to Alpha

Undoubtedly all you fraternity and sorority folks and some of you Athenian-types will recognize those words as the ending and beginning letters of the Greek alphabet. Hopefully, a number of you will recognize the inference to Jesus being the beginning and end of all things as well. In the Bible it says, "I am the Alpha and the Omega, the First and the Last, the Beginning and the End" (Revelation 22:13 NLT). So you are probably wondering why I've turned it around? Why the Omega to the Alpha? Here's the simple answer: because you need to know where you plan to end up to know how to work back to where you are now. Remember the "YOU ARE HERE" sign at the mall? Same principle! You have to know the end goal to head towards it, and you have to know where you are now to know where to begin. This book is actually structured that way. I told you the good stuff up front of how Jesus stepped into my totally messed up life and pointed me in the right direction. I was completely lost and had no idea where I was heading. I was a ship afloat and had no compass or map or GPS to find my way anywhere.

There's another interesting dimension to this "omega to alpha" phenomenon. God wants to take you from where your life went off course back to a fresh start. A "do-over." Only God actually knows what He planned for you and where you are supposed to end up, so only He can truly head you in the right direction and guarantee your final destination. Isaiah spells that out exactly: "Declaring the end from the beginning, And from ancient times things which have not been done, Saying, 'My plan will be established, And I will accomplish all My good pleasure'" (Isaiah 46:10 NASB). He is our eternal compass. You may recall that Jesus gave me a Bible verse to remember that first day with Him on the balcony: "'For I know the plans I have for you,' declares the LORD, 'plans to prosper you and not to harm you, to give you a future and a hope'" (Jeremiah 29:11 NIV). The King James Bible version of that verse says it this way, "For I know the thoughts that I think toward you, saith the LORD, thoughts of peace, and not of evil, to give you an expected end." Wow, an *expected end*. God knows your ending from the beginning, and He fully expects you to make it there.

It may surprise some of you that God is actually expecting you to finish in a prosperous place that happens to be called heaven. The good news is that He is making every provision for that to happen. We just have to let Him into our messy lives and start leading us in the right direction towards that end. Without trying to make you dizzy, spinning you around, let's start figuring out just where you are, how you got there, when you may have gone off course, and how to start heading in the right direction.

You already know that there are numerous viewpoints about each of those questions and each person, including you, have perspectives on how you got to where you are today. Each event of your life has an impact on how you look at life, and unless you live in a bubble, lots of people have influenced each of those events as well. So the question ultimately becomes, "What's your truth?" Is your life heading in the direction you want to go? Do you feel like you are fulfilling your life's purpose? Do you need a do-over? Do you need a divine date with Jesus? I'm waging a bet that if you are reading this book, you probably need the do-over and the date. Jesus definitely has the compass for your life, and He's ready anytime you are. So let's take a closer look at your present circumstances.

Since you are made up of a spirit, soul, and body, we will look at where you are on the happiness scale for each aspect. Do you feel that your body is fearfully and wonderfully made? Do you believe your body is a temple for the Holy Spirit? Do you believe you have the mind of Christ? Since your soul consists of your thoughts, emotions, and free will, let's check on how you are doing with each of those. Are your thoughts fixed on what is true, and honorable, and right, and pure, and lovely, and admirable? Do you think about things that are excellent and worthy of praise? Are you filled with peace, love, joy, patience, and self-control? Have you made all righteous decisions? Well, if you are like most of us, probably not. Let's not forget to check in on your spirit. Umm, have you ever checked in on your spirit? Do you think you are filled with the Holy Spirit? Do you know who the Holy Spirit is? Do you believe you have a spirit? So on a scale of 1 to 10 how happy are you with how you are doing in your spirit, soul, and body? Regardless of what that number is, Jesus can take you higher.

If, however, you're really struggling with your level of happiness, Jesus wants to take you by the hand and lead you each step of the way to a place where you are filled with love, joy, abundant happiness, and hope every day of your life. To do that, you're going to have to trust that He really does know the way, and He always tells the truth. How do I know that? I and several other million Christians believe that the Holy Bible is the God-breathed truth. The Bible is the indisputable word of God. When we walk by the wisdom of the Word of God, then we are essentially holding Jesus' hand and letting Him guide us in each and every circumstance of our lives. We allow Jesus'

> *Jesus wants to take you by the hand and lead you each step of the way to a place where you are filled with love, joy, and abundant happiness, and hope*

love to be the guiding light that directs our every step. I'm not trying to be poetic here. I'm actually speaking of everyday practical guidance for how to walk in love, joy, peace, and an incredible bliss. I'm a living testimony that it works, and that's coming from someone who didn't recognize a chapter or verse of the Bible when she took her first step of faith in Jesus' loving guidance.

And let me remind you that I still don't consider the Bible a religion book. It's so, so much more. When you start to believe what Jesus thinks about you, you will stop letting the world tell you who you are and what you are capable of. You will look through a clear lens of love and see the magnificent future that God had planned for you all along. You will walk in confidence knowing that all things are possible with God, and you will do incredible exploits. I want to instill in you a triumphant spirit and faith because I know God didn't create anything that He didn't plan to be magnificent. You, my friend, are magnificent—even if you are having a hard time believing that right now. I want to show you how to start trading any lies you may be believing about yourself for the truth that God says about you. The Bible calls that transforming your mind, but honestly, it is just trading the lies the world may have made you believe for God's truth about you.

Dispelling the Lies

There are so many ways that our view of ourselves gets distorted throughout our lives. It can seem as though we are walking around in a carnival house of mirrors. Too skinny, too wide, too tall, too short; our image gets distorted by the image we are trying to mirror. We often adopt whatever the current fad is in our society for how we see or feel about ourselves and our lives. What constitutes success, beauty, happiness, and fulfillment are usually based on what we see or perceive in the world around us. What part of the country or world we live in greatly dictates what we must achieve to be really happy, but that may not actually produce happiness in us. Why not? Because those measurement ideals are usually only external aspects of our physical world and seldom take into consideration the soul or spiritual parts of us. Parts of ourselves are left hungry and wanting.

We often hear people say I need something to feed my soul, and they would be right. However, we often interchange the words soul and spirit or completely overlook our actual spirit. As previously described, our souls contain our emotions, thoughts, and free will, whereas our spirit is what is breathed into us by God. It is our connection to God. What people are trying to convey when they say they need to feed their souls usually means that they need something that their spirit can identify with or that makes them feel alive. That inner, unseen part of them that longs for something that brings fulfillment, wholeness, purpose, and meaning to their lives. They want their spirits to come alive. But since your spirit is unseen in the physical world, it's very difficult to get in touch with that part of ourselves or to know exactly how we feed that part of our being.

There are countless books and movements that tout increased spirituality, but not all of them point you to God or Jesus. You are not galactic particles that just happened to land on earth.

You are not just positive and negatively charged ions. You are not just a carbon footprint in time. You are a masterpiece created for such a time as this. No one is exactly like you, and no one can fulfill the part of destiny that is held within your life. You have a purpose that was written for you alone in your DNA. That makes you pretty darn special.

If you have never thought of yourself as a masterpiece, that may sound foreign or even completely opposite of how you view yourself. Usually, those who see themselves as that would be classified as "full of themselves" or just plain prideful, and that would be true if they thought everything they have accomplished was through their own doing or strength. But I'm talking about how God sees you and the perfect plan He has made for you. You know I don't think I've ever realized just how often Jeremiah 29:11 regarding God's plans for me was operating in my life, and you may not either. And there's more to it than that; every Bible verse is true and working in our lives every day through all of eternity. That may really come as a surprise to some of you.

See if any of these statements resonate with you. You are loved with an everlasting love. You are victorious. You are chosen. You are an overcomer. You are more than a conqueror. You are beloved. If any of those statements are not resonating with you then you are being deceived because those are all biblical truths about you. So, where is the disconnect, and how do we dispel the lies we are believing about ourselves? That would be where our soul comes into play; our mind (thoughts), emotions (feelings), and our free will choices along with our day-to-day life experiences heavily influence what we believe about ourselves and coincidentally how we assume others think about us as well. Now that can surely be a double-edged sword if ever I saw one.

"We are told in the living Word (Bible) that God's thoughts toward us are as numerous as the grains of sand upon the earth. This has been mathematically calculated as seven quintillions, but really, the analogy means immeasurable. We are so important and beloved that He can't stop thinking of us."[2] That is a lot of thinking about us on God's part, yet we tend to judge ourselves by a handful of people in our sphere of influence. The tough part is trying to believe what God says over what we have come to believe about ourselves. Why in the world do we hang onto the lies? Often they are hurtful, painful, and downright miserable. Exactly! That is exactly why we hang onto those things, or more correctly, they hang onto us. Our spiritual hearts get wounded by the hurtful things that are either said or happen to us. They can pierce both our physical and spiritual selves and leave us wounded and confused about our perspective on the world and the place we hold in it.

As a child, you may have heard the old nursery rhyme, "Sticks and stones may break my bones, but words will never hurt me."[3] Oh, that this was true, but sadly, it couldn't be further

---

[2] "God Thinks Of Us, Continually" Inspirational Christian Blogs by CherylZ 1961 on JULY 31, 2015. Retrieved from: https://www.inspirationalchristianblogs.com/2015/07/31/god-thinks-of-us-continually/. Accessed 8 February 2021.

[3] "Sticks and Stones" is an English-language children's rhyme. The rhyme is used as a defense against name-calling and verbal bullying, intended to increase resiliency, avoid physical retaliation and to remain calm and good-living. Retrieved from: https://en.wikipedia.org/wiki/Sticks_and_Stones; Accessed 10 February 2021.

from the truth. Anyone who has ever been on the receiving end of a cutting-edge comment knows just how hurtful words can be. Their sting can last for decades and wound souls and spirits equally long. Caustic words equate to spiritual bullying. The degree to which they wound is in direct relation to how much you care about that person's opinion or affection or how much you may already actually believe the harsh comment. In many cases wounding comments happen very early in life. They can be intentional or totally unintentional but harmful all the same. Our parents seldom realize how damaging their verbal assessments of us shape our opinions of ourselves. That probably doesn't come as a surprise to any of you but it does lay the groundwork for our fledgling image of ourselves and opens the door for more bruising.

It is fairly normative that each family has a highly favored child, and if there is more than one sibling in the household, consequently, there is a less or least favored child as well. Middle children, you have my commiseration. High praise equates to being well-loved, while lesser comparisons leave us wanting in the "loved" department. Love and acceptance are requirements for a healthy self-assessment. Our parents reign foremost in that department well into our adult lives. What they think of us literally forms what we think of ourselves. As we grow older, what others outside our family members think of us markedly impacts our feeling loved quotient as well. Throughout our lives, other people's opinions of us affect our self-image to varying degrees. Words have an immense impact on our oh-so-fragile self-worth.

Doubtless, we have all been hurt spiritually in countless ways. Whenever love is withheld in some way, it results in rejection and damage to our hearts and inner selves. As I have already said, you were made in God's image, and God is love. Love is the one thing we need and desire more than any other single thing in our entire lives. Without it, we shrivel up and cease to function. That is why solitary confinement in prison is the most dire of punishments. All human contact is withheld, the ultimate human rejection, and literally, your spirit begins to die. We are made for love, by love, and to be loved, and without it, we cannot thrive. This is why knowing a loving God is so critical to our lives in every way. For when we know without a doubt that we are loved, we blossom and flourish.

It stands to reason, then, that to adjust our thinking we need to adjust who we are letting formulate our self-worth and feeling of being fully loved. It's not a far leap to figure out that we need to allow God's love to override whatever false image we hold of ourselves to start to dispel the lies that have seeded themselves in our wounded hearts and minds. The voices that we allow into our hearts will either help us or hurt us. Whoever we open the door to and allow to impact our self-image plays a major role in how we rectify the true image we were created in. The world will most certainly impact our image of ourselves, but it does not have to control it. You were given free will, and that is your ticket to deciding whose appraisal of you you want to accept.

If you have ever attended a wedding, you more than likely have heard some part of this passage: "Love is patient, love is kind. It does not envy; it does not boast: it is not proud.

It is not rude: it is not self-seeking, it is not easily angered, it keeps no account of wrongs. Love takes no pleasure in evil but rejoices in the truth. It bears all things, believes all things, hopes all things, endures all things. Love never fails." (1 Corinthians 13). Needless to say, those are some powerful words and even more powerful ideals. If what you are hearing or believing about yourself does not line up with those verses, then it probably isn't very loving or stemming from love. Here are a few more synonyms for love. See if any of these ring a bell for you. Love is: devotion, ardor, fidelity, fondness, cherished, passionate, zealous, respectful, adored, captivating, delightful, dear, treasured, esteemed, and altogether lovely. Those are the feelings God has for you. Yes, you!

I realize that few of us feel we are living under such heavenly adulation, but it doesn't change the fact that God never stops feeling that way about us. He knows the "real" us. He knows who He created each and every one of us to be and then created the plan for us to achieve it. That plan is not hidden away in heaven, it's right here, right now, and as I said, you already have the ticket to possess it. Your gift of free will allows you access to God's incredible plan for your life. You just have to understand what an incredible ticket it really is and start to use it the way it was designed to work.

Let's try a few ticket examples to illustrate how this all works. It's really not as difficult as you may think. Imagine yourself at one of the huge amusement parks. You've purchased your entrance ticket and you have free access to ride all the rides as often as you would like. At each ride there are usually multiple lines you can choose to enter as you wind your way through the waiting maze till you reach the ride entry point. Two of the lines wind back and forth, each taking different amounts of time to progress through. We will call the line you chose to enter as the godly one because it aligns with godly, biblical principles. But as you slowly move along, you notice that the other line is moving faster so you duck under the rope and jump into the other line. Hey, I've seen it; everybody does it; don't try to deny it. However, this line has a slightly different name. It's the not-so-godly line. It is the line of self-satisfaction instead of godly satisfaction. This is the line that takes you out of alignment with God and puts you in opposition to Him. Every time you choose something that isn't "in line" with what God says, you literally slip under the line into unrighteousness which, dare I say it, is actually sin. But suddenly, you notice there are a couple of people running up the third line flying right by both other lines. Where are they going, and how come they are getting to ride way ahead of everybody else? That, my friends, is the fast-pass line. Every time we freely choose to act selflessly, as Jesus did, we get a fast-pass to every incredible thing God has in store for us.

Our free will ticket allows us to choose how we align ourselves literally with every decision we make every single day of our lives. We get to choose how we act, believe, or not believe about everything that comes our way. Choosing to stay in line with what God says is right and good will always get us to the end goal. Choosing to come out of line with God's ways always takes us longer and further away from the end goal. That line only appeared to be moving faster, but the truth is that it branched off to the left somewhere along the line and takes you a lot longer to actually get to the finish line. But thankfully for us, God keeps weaving our path back to Him, and He gives us the ultimate fast-pass option ever purchased, and that's Jesus.

So what does this all have to do with love? It has everything to do with love because of Jesus' totally selfless sacrifice on the cross when He chose to die for our sins to be reconciled to God while we were yet sinners. God's fast-pass is Jesus Christ. He paid the price and bought us a ticket to eternal life for no other reason than His love for us, and there's nothing religious about that. It's patient, kind, not envious, boastful, or proud. It is not rude, self-seeking, easily angered, or counting up wrongs. It took no pleasure in evil but rejoiced in the truth. It bore all things, believed all things, hoped all things, and endured all things[4] just for you and me. Now that's some kind of love!

Each of us has a choice to choose love over offense, obedience over sin, forgiveness over bitterness, and God's way over our way. None of these are difficult words to understand, but when our hearts have been wounded, they become much more difficult to actually do. Our hearts and spirits need to be mended so we can see ourselves and our lives through Jesus' eyes and believe the glorious plan that God has for our lives because all things are possible with God.[5]

---

[4] Paraphrased 1 Corinthians 13:4-7 BSB. "Love is patient, love is kind. It does not envy, it does not boast, it is not proud. It is not rude, it is not self-seeking, it is not easily angered, it keeps no account of wrongs. Love takes no pleasure in evil, but rejoices in the truth. It bears all things, believes all things, hopes all things, endures all things."

[5] Paraphrase of Mark 10:27 NIV.

Mending Hearts and Spirits

I want to tell you a little bit about my own journey of mending my heart and spirit. You will recall that my father was very physically abusive. The beatings lasted all the way into my teen years when grievously, the belt was traded in for fists. The beatings were fierce and traumatic. I dreaded living in that house and couldn't wait till I could leave for college. I paid my own way through college and chose a college over three hours away, so I seldom had to come home. I had a built in excuse to avoid my detestable home life. When my father finally passed away, I didn't cry, I was relieved. I was the last one to leave the gravesite because I needed to see him buried in the ground to know he could never hurt me again. Then I cried, but I didn't forgive him. What he had done for all those years was criminal. Today he would have been put in jail, but back then, it wasn't a crime, and there was no legal action ever taken. The grief I carried for many years was for a childhood gone wrong—an innocence lost.

Regrettably, things didn't go well in my married life either so my spiritual wounds stayed open and only grew deeper and profoundly abysmal. Both my spirit and my soul were tortured, bruised, and severely afflicted. Certainly, neither healing nor mending came with his death. Forgiveness was not in my heart or spirit. I was the one who was wounded, and I had a right to be angry and bitter. I was wronged, bitterly wronged. Healing was a long way off, and my soul and spirit wounds stayed gapingly open. Another life gone wrong, dreadfully, dreadfully wrong. I could not grieve my husband's death either, and the pain in my heart seemed endless, completely bottomless. My spirit was tormented night and day. There was no rest for the weary and the night terrors of my childhood continued into my adult life. Sleep was not my friend. It only brought forth more fear and more dread. No matter how hard I tried, I could not seem to escape the terror of my life, even in their deaths.

Until I was confronted with the fact that until I could find forgiveness in my heart for both my father and my husband, I was not going to be free of the torment. Healing only truly happens when love enters our hearts. I surely had not received love in the physical world, so I had to go to the one place I had ever experienced real love, yup that's right—Jesus. Jesus is still the answer to every problem; He always was and always will be.

There is a process aptly named Inner Healing that provides a means to walk through that forgiveness process allowing for forgiveness, repentance, and the substituting of truth for lies that have pervaded our minds and hearts. We invite Jesus to enter into the process and hold us secure as we hand Him all our hurts, disappointments, fears, wounds, anxieties, mistrust, suffering, unhappiness, grief, loss, trouble, confusion, mistakes, abuse, sadness, harm, duress, pain and any other condition that we need to be released from. We hand it all over to Him and ask Him to exchange them for the opposite facet of each. Jesus trades us love, joy, peace, patience, kindness, goodness, faithfulness, gentleness, and self-control instead.[6] In essence, He infuses us with His Spirit. Once we are filled with the fullness

---

[6] Galatians 5:22-23 ESV "But the fruit of the Spirit is love, joy, peace, patience, kindness, goodness, faithfulness, gentleness, self-control; against such things there is no law."

of His love, there is a catharsis that happens that enables us to release the hurts and allows for forgiveness to flow through our hearts.

Some hurts are so deep and long-lived that it really is only possible to find forgiveness in our hearts with Jesus' help. When we are able to release the wounds from our spirits and souls, we can ask Jesus to make known to us what lies we have believed because of the hurtful things that have been said or done to us throughout our lives. What things have we believed that are not the truth of who we are in His eyes? What things do not align with His Holy Bible truths? We can ask Him to tell us the truth about each of these false beliefs so that the wounds can be erased from our hearts and minds. Then as we choose to receive Jesus' truths, we can turn from the lies we have believed and walk in a renewed way of thinking about all those past experiences. We turn from our old ways of thinking and start living into the new and correct image of who we are. When at last we are able to recognize the error in our old ways of thinking, we can apologize to Jesus for ever doubting His truth. That is known as repentance.

Once I had gone through this process, I found forgiveness for both my father and husband. I will confess that it took time, and I wasn't instantly able to release some of the really heinous things that cut me to the bone with painful memories. Years upon years upon years of hurts take time to mend. They take time to address and process. Be kind to yourself as you go through the process.

However, this story still isn't over. I still suffered from night terrors of the memories of these awful experiences and the torments still in my soul. I suffered from night terrors from the time I was 15 years old until I was 59—that's 44 years! My emotions had healed, but my thoughts were still plagued with fearful images. As a matter of explanation night terrors are different from nightmares. Night terrors involve just that—terror. Extreme fear, anxiety, and distress during sleep. Nightmares are unpleasant or frightening dreams that cause emotional distress but don't always involve the level of terror that night terrors do. Neither are desirable, I can assure you. The only remedy that I knew was to work myself to utter and total exhaustion so that I might find a few hours of rest.

I eventually discovered that the trauma I had experienced in many of my beatings and sexual assaults opened doors in my spirit that allowed for tormenting spirits to enter in. These spirits, just as their name implies, torment you in your thoughts and dreams. They are relentless and absolutely without compassion. My healing process still needed deliverance from the numerous traumas I had experienced. Hurt and trauma are not the same. A traumatic experience generally happens when you are involved with a life-threatening experience, or you witness a death-related event. Clinically this is diagnosed as Post Traumatic Stress Disorder[7] or PTSD. It is frequently associated with military veterans that have witnessed horrific

---

[7] "Post Traumatic Stress Disorder" The Center for Treatment of Anxiety and Mood Disorders; Post-Traumatic Stress Disorder; What is Trauma; Retrieved from: https://centerforanxietydisorders.com/what-is-trauma/#:~:text=In%20 general%2C%20trauma%20can%20be,is%20deeply%20distressing%20 or%20disturbing.

war scenes or felt their lives in imminent danger, but it is equally debilitating for anyone faced with a life-threatening situation.

I sought professional counseling for several years, dealing with the myriad of traumatic experiences I had suffered during those 44 years. I did unearth many of the causes and was able to manage the physical triggers that often had me running for cover, but I could not seem to get them to stop. I didn't want to spend the rest of my life battling to manage my night terrors; I wanted to be healed and free of them.

Finally, in the summer of 2016, I found permanent relief from this beastly disruption of my daily life through a deliverance prayer model[8] developed by Dr. Mike Hutchings. He is currently the Director of Education for Global Awakening, an evangelistic ministry in Mechanicsburg, PA. He directs Dr. Randy Clark's Global School of Supernatural Ministry and the Global Certification Programs. While training at Global Awakening, I underwent the Post-Traumatic Stress Disorder (PTSD) deliverance prayer process that combines each of the steps we have discussed thus far by inviting Jesus into each part of our tortured spirit, soul, and body to bring the wholeness that only He can. After 44 years of night terrors, I finally slept a whole night free from torment and haven't been tormented since! Praise God, Hallelujah!

I will be forever grateful to Dr. Hutchings for developing this trauma deliverance prayer model and to Jesus for restoring peace to all of me. The point I want to drive home is that we

---

[8] Mike Hutchings, *Supernatural Freedom from the Captivity of Trauma* (Shippensburg, PA: Destiny Image Publishers, Inc. 2021, pp. 157-172).

must address both our physical maladies as well as the spiritual components that are driving and exasperating them. In addition to Christian counseling for Inner Healing, I encourage the reader to seek spiritual deliverance to find real and lasting peace.

All true deliverance is a process. It takes time to walk back through the events of your life that initiated the woundings, subsequent issues, and painful torment. It is not enough to only track the initial causes and develop management strategies, but the ultimate goal should be lasting healing. Only Jesus can do that for you. Better still, He wants to free you from all the bondages that hold and scourge your heart and soul. That freedom only comes from the inside out. When you can determine the original problem, reject the lies, close the doors of entry, seek forgiveness for yourself and grant forgiveness to the offending person, and walk in your true God-given identity, you will be able to regain your life and successfully accomplish the final step of your deliverance by kicking every tormenting, lying spirit to the curb. This is true freedom.

What is Your True Identity?

You may be wondering why I have qualified identity with the adjective true? Because if you have been living under a false assessment of your self-worth, you will need to adjust your beliefs and behaviors. If, for instance, you have felt unlovable, you will have constantly made decisions based on that value judgment and sought affirmation in a myriad of unhealthy ways. It is easy to fall prey to perfectionism, manipulation, and promiscuity, just to name a few. If you have felt unworthy, you may never have established any healthy boundaries. Your kindness and generosity may have been taken advantage of, or you may have been walked all over and taken for granted. Setting self-respecting boundaries will be essential to walk with self-respect. If you have felt unsuccessful, unlikable, undeserving, unsuitable, unbecoming, "un" anything, you will need to trade those beliefs for the things that God has established as truth about who you are.

This is where you get to choose the kind and color of glasses you are looking through. Slip the collar **Trade the lies** off whoever has been holding your leash. **you have been** Trade the lies you have been believing for God's truth. Mend your bruised heart, and **believing for** lean into the hundreds of promises and **God's truth** blessings God has been holding just for you. Your true identity only comes from one place, and that is God. He is the only one who knows exactly who you are—spirit, soul, and body. He knew you before you were ever even born. He created you in His image, and He didn't make any mistakes, or change His mind about you or put anything bad into you. He made you to shine and to love and to be loved. The essence of who you are, your spirit, is absolutely lovely, lovable, and beautiful.

Chapter 4

Putting the Pieces Back Together Again

Polar Blast

"Really, God! I can't believe you are doing this to me." I cried from a nearly healed heart that cold January night of 2011. I cried that just as I grabbed my right ankle as both my fibula and tibia bones in my lower leg tried to break through the skin as I crumbled to the ground. I heard the crystal-clear, crisp snap of my bones as my foot twisted in a direction that God never intended for it to move in. It was nine months after my husband's death, and I was just starting to feel like I was able to face the world again and try to regain a "normal" life.

I decided to head to the gym right after work that day. It was only a little over a block away, so I could just leave my car parked at work and scoot up the back alley to the gym. As a staff member of the University, I had full privileges to work out at the beautifully equipped and super convenient facility. It had been a gorgeous sunny winter day. The sun had warmed the ground and the snow melted under its warm rays. That was right up to the minute the polar vortex plummeted the temperature back down below freezing in just a matter of minutes. A freak polar air blast hit our little University town and created a hidden minefield of black ice everywhere. One minute I was walking enthusiastically along, and the next I was a wailing human heap on the ground.

"Honestly, God, I was just finally feeling a little bit of happiness, and boom! I'm writhing around in astronomical pain on the freezing ground!" Needless to say, I was screaming as well. It was already dark, but there were still students walking around campus, and one quickly came to my rescue—well, sort of. He was a tall, dark young man in a long black wool coat. I yelled frantically, "I broke my leg; I broke my leg. Please call 911!" This surely didn't seem like a difficult concept, but the young man just kept looking at me. I screamed with a lot more anger and frustration in my voice, "Call 911, call 911, I need an ambulance!" But the young man just shook his head; he didn't understand. *How was that possible?* But then he tried to respond to my yelling, and in a moment, I realized that he was speaking another language, and he actually didn't understand what I was saying or what had happened. In an incredibly desperate plea, I asked him if he had a cell phone and made the motion of putting a phone to my ear. He shook his head and pulled out his phone. He handed it to me, and I called 911. As I explained what had happened, an ambulance was dispatched. I handed the phone back to the worried young man.

"God, you've got to be kidding me. *Really?* I had to make the 911 call myself? What have I done to deserve this?" My mind was a jumble of pain, fear, confusion, anger, freezing; there was a lot of freezing, come to think of it. The whole polar vortex thing had plummeted the temperatures to well below freezing, and I only had light workout clothes on; no coat, hat, or gloves. My whole body was shaking violently now, and the pain was by far the most excruciating pain I had ever experienced. When you are in such pain, your body goes into a protective mode known as shock, and time seems to stand still. Minutes seem like hours. *Where could that ambulance be?* The whole campus only takes five minutes to drive across. Lots of on-lookers had gathered by now, but there was nothing they could do to help but wait and watch.

What I didn't know then was that ten other people had broken their legs that same night in the same few minutes after the polar air blast hit our campus. The ambulance didn't arrive for nearly twenty minutes which in "shock time" was very close to an eternity. What I also did not know was that the bone breaking was actually going to prove to be the least of my worries. Hard to imagine that, but it's true. If you are like most of the average population, you probably thought like I did. *I just have to hold on till I get to the hospital, the doctors will come running, I'll be in surgery in minutes, and I'll wake up, and everything will be fine.* Cut to commercial. Nope, turns out it doesn't work that way. All the doctors were already in surgery, and I had to wait until four o'clock the following afternoon for an available operating room! Eternity couldn't come fast enough.

One metal plate and thirteen titanium screws later, and my leg was fixed. Fast forward two days, and I'm taking another ride in the ambulance. Seems blood clots can be a dangerous result of surgery, especially the ones that pass through your heart into your lungs. Those are the ones that can kill you! Thankfully, I'm still here to talk about it. Fast forward a couple of months, and you guessed it, I'm heading back to the hospital yet again. At least this time, it was not in the ambulance. This time, the blood clot spanned the whole length of my leg from my calf clear up to my groin. After the ultrasound, five doctors were waiting for me in the ER. They looked back and forth at each other, trying to see who had the nerve in their eyes to tell me the prognosis. I knew this wasn't going to be good, but I truly wasn't prepared for what they had to say.

"If the clot moves, there's nothing we will be able to do to save you. Your condition is life-threatening. You're going to need surgery as soon as possible to remove the clot." Bam! Did not see that coming. All I could think about was my daughters. First, they lost their dad, and now they were going to lose their mom. *How was this even possible? What about all those promises, God? Did you save me just to off me? What kind of cruel joke is this?* A different kind of shock set in, but before I had a chance to even start shaking, I was whisked away for more ultrasounds and blood tests. The pulmonary surgeon was scheduled as was the operating room. There really was no time to lose.

Well, it doesn't take a brain surgeon to figure out that since I'm still writing, the clot didn't move but what happened next defies, well, everything. After the carotid artery ultrasound and a brain scan, I was taken to a room and prepped for surgery. I was given some drugs to calm me down. An IV with Heparin[1] medication was started, and I just had to wait for the pulmonary surgeon to arrive. In fairly short order, the surgeon arrived and told me we would be going into surgery in just a bit; however, about ten minutes later, he came back and informed me that there had been a serious car accident and he would have to attend to the crash victims first, but I was on deck for surgery immediately after that. Slow forward several hours, and the surgeon returned and said I would be heading into surgery as soon as the operating room was ready to receive me. Minutes later, the nurse informed me there had been a second car accident, and the surgeon would have to tend to those victims before me. *Really God?*

So why have I dragged this story out for so many pages? Because sometimes, we just don't understand what God is up to when it looks like everything possible is working against us. But God does have a plan, and it seldom looks like what we think it should look like. Mostly because we don't usually

---

[1] "Heparin" is an anticoagulant (blood thinner) that prevents the formation of blood clots. Heparin is used to treat and prevent blood clots caused by certain medical conditions or medical procedures. It is also used before surgery to reduce the risk of blood clots. Retrieved from: www.drugs.com. Accessed 16 February 2021.

recognize a miracle until it's blatantly and undeniably right in front of us. Spoiler alert: the surgery never happened! Cut to finale. The surgeon worked through the night on the car crash victims, and when he came and checked on me in the morning, miraculously, all the swelling had gone down in my leg, and when they sent me for another ultrasound, the clot had completely disappeared! The clot that should have killed me was gone! The hematologist confirmed that there was no medical explanation for that happening. The Heparin certainly would have helped, but as a slow functioning drug could not have accounted for the total disappearance of such a massive clot. Enter stage right: Undeniable miracle!

Sometimes God not only surprises us, He blows us away. Again I had to rearrange everything I knew about God. Even though I had met the unbelievably loving Jesus, I still struggled to comprehend the plans God had for my life. Again I had come face-to-face with the miraculous. As I have mentioned previously, when you are faced with a life-threatening event, you're changed. You can be traumatized, or sometimes you find God in all the confusion. I felt like I was in the fender bender scenario again as my mind struggled to catch hold of any of the innumerable questions flying by in my mind. *What just happened? How is this possible? Am I actually going to be okay? What are you doing, God? Can I go home now? How are the other people from the accidents? Can I please talk to a doctor? Can I please talk to a priest? Are you sure?* These questions and hundreds more pelted my mind like a semi-automatic BB gun? Is that even a thing? The truth is that absolutely no answers were forthcoming, and I found myself in a state of mental, physical, and spiritual exhaustion. Now what?

Now what indeed? When you come face to face with your own mortality, it's absolutely frightening. When you truly believe you may actually die in the very immediate future, a lot changes inside of you. Most of the things you have worried about in the world instantly fade away. After you wonder if it's going to hurt, your thoughts go to the most important things of your life: your loved ones and your hereafter. You worry if your loved ones are going to be okay without you. Have you secured a sound future for them? Is everything in order? Sometimes you don't even have that much time, but in the midst of everything happening at that moment, there is a split second when you wonder, *Am I going up or down? Is there really a heaven and a hell?*

If you are blessed and narrowly escape the clutches of the Grim Reaper, you start to ask yourself a lot of very serious questions. There comes an enormous reordering of priorities in your life, and depending on your age and state of health, you get busy setting things in "right" order, right quick! If you are a believing man or woman, you thank God for your blessing of extra time. If not, you just thank your lucky stars that you made that narrow escape, and your mind may just sneak a peek at the possibility of there actually being a God. Often "Bucket Lists"[2] materialize as a result of your near miss. No matter how you initially process facing your mortality, at some point, you

[2] "Bucket list" Wikipedia: A list of activities to do before dying ("kick the bucket"). Retrieved from: https://en.wikipedia.org/wiki/Bucket_list. Accessed 17 February 2021.

eventually sit down and really look your life over. *Was it what I really wanted? Did I do all the things I wanted to do? Did I make a difference or at least leave a mark on this world? Could I have done things differently? Did I do a good job at _____?* (You fill in the blank).

I most certainly underwent this process after my second near-miss event. I hadn't really understood the actual consequences with the first blood clot episode, so this process didn't happen for me until the doctors made it abundantly clear to me the second time around. I was actually pretty angry with God about this whole second episode. *Hadn't I been through enough already? Hadn't my suffering been sufficient to give me a pass for a while? Wasn't the astronomical pain I was in night and day from my broken ankle enough to satisfy some necessary level of repentance? Why could He possibly still need me to suffer?* Admittedly, not the most gratitude-filled responses I could have had.

> Somehow I had managed to move into a loving relationship with Jesus, but I still held the belief that God the Father was a vengeful God

What I didn't know yet was that my old religious beliefs still held me bound to a God of fear and anger. I still hadn't reckoned my faith beliefs, and I totally missed the God of mercy and second, third and fourth chances. Somehow I had managed to move into a loving relationship with Jesus, but I still held the belief that God the Father was a vengeful God. I just hadn't truly grasped the whole three-in-one godhead thing yet. Changing fifty years of beliefs just doesn't happen overnight. It's a process, and old habits die hard. I was blaming God for the problems I was having but completely missing the fact that I had received repeated miracles of healing. How do you miss that? The actual fact was, as stated in Genesis 50:20, that even though the enemy planned evil against me, God planned it for good to bring about the present result—the survival of many people. I was a benefactor of one of those plans for my good, my survival, and not my harm. I finally realized why Jesus had told me in that very first encounter to remember Jeremiah 29:11, that God's plans were to prosper me and not harm me. How quickly we forget!

I was starting to feel like a cat with nine lives, but I was using them up pretty quickly at this rate. After the second round of blood clots, I was extremely weak and needed a wheelchair to get around because I didn't even have the strength to use crutches. I was certainly slowed down, and I figured I had better start to have that life review now: Get out of my family home … Check. Go to college … Check. Get married … Check. Have kids … Check. Buy a horse farm … Check, check. Live happily ever after … Umm-not so far. In my frustration to understand how everything had gotten so far off track, I started my inquisition of God.

"God, if your plans really are to prosper me and not to harm me, how come I'm in this wheelchair, and my life has taken another really bad turn? What gives?" I followed this question with a non-stop litany of equally baffled questions until I ran out of steam. Then in a very calm and matter-of-fact tone, God answered me, "Be still and know that I am God."[3] Well, that certainly wasn't the answer I needed, wanted, or expected. So I reiterated a second round of the same questions but worded slightly differently. Perhaps God missed what I was aiming for, and if I rephrased them just a bit, God would be much more forthcoming with the requisite answers. Nope! "Be still and know that I am God" was all I got back. This was not going well, or at least not anywhere fast. Not to be brushed off so easily, I riddled God again and again with endless questions. And God being the patient God that He is just answered again and again, "Be still and know that I am God."

Just for the record, God's answer remained the same for the next six months. No matter the question, the answer was always the same: "Be still and know that I am God." Clearly, this was a test of wills but even though it took me a really long time to figure it out, God always wins that battle. And with little else I could do, I finally succumbed and was still. Also, for the record, I don't do "still" well. I prefer life at a hundred miles an hour, thank you. Which was actually my survival mechanism for avoiding the oft times bleak truth of my life, but God wanted me to slow down and look my life over, and He wanted to be God for me. I just had no idea what that looked like or how it worked because I didn't know God. I feared Him, but I knew very little about Him, and He wanted to change that for me. Now He wanted me to trust Him. I just never realized how big such a small word could be.

---

[3] Psalm 46:10 NIV "He says, 'Be still, and know that I am God; I will be exalted among the nations, I will be exalted in the earth.'"

Trust

T-R-U-S-T just five letters, but they proved to be some of the most frightening letters I had ever tackled. A quick Google search produces the definition of trust as "a firm belief in the reliability, truth, ability, or strength of someone or something." I didn't have to read very far to see my problem: a firm belief. My firm belief was that God was angry and vengeful, so how could I trust someone who was angry and vengeful? I saw how well that worked out with my earthly father, and that wasn't exactly ideal. Didn't work out too great with my husband either. I was in a trust dilemma. Jesus was great; I trusted Him just fine, but God not so much. So, where exactly was the disconnect? The disconnect was in the same place I found it the first time—religion. Religion had taught me to fear God (which incidentally isn't entirely bad), but my knowledge was so rudimentary because fifty years ago, only the priests handled the Bible. I didn't know God because I didn't know the vast information contained in the Bible. Back to square one again.

Religion had gotten in the way of understanding who God actually was to me. I know that the nuns and priests were trying their best to teach me about God, but the whole part about love just kept falling through the cracks in their Bibles. Hell seemed to preoccupy most of the teaching, and that only served to push me away in fear. So, now this fearsome God wanted me to sit quietly and trust Him. Trust Him to do what? Now that was a scary question all by itself, let alone trying to figure out how still is still and where I was supposed to get the knowing part. But being laid up with my ankle still not healed and my lungs still healing from the blood clots that had weakened them, I had nothing better to do than be still and wait for God to say something… anything!

Eventually, I figured out all by myself that God did a lot of talking in the Bible, so I started to spend time browsing about in the Bible. "Browsing" being the functional word here. I didn't know that there were study Bibles or even Bible studies which I now know are two different things. I just flipped around mostly in the New Testament to the parables that I had heard on Sunday mornings that weren't too scary. Then one day, pretty much by accident, I came across the verse that says, "My people are destroyed for lack of knowledge" (Hosea 4:6 NIV). A little light finally went off in my head that the destruction in my life had a lot to do with the fact that I didn't know God. I've learned a lot since that day.

The Bible can be a pretty overwhelming book to read, and understanding doesn't just happen overnight, but it contains the most essential knowledge in the world for living an abundant life and finding out just who God really is. Since I am really lousy at the being still part, I decided to ask Jesus to help me learn about God. Sounds downright silly now that I think about it, but that's exactly how I started out. I trusted Jesus, and I knew He knew more about God the Father than anybody else. So every day I peppered Jesus with endless questions about God and heaven and what all that stuff in the Bible really meant. I had only learned the most basic surface meanings recorded in the Bible but soon learned that there were much deeper meanings to everything. God is surely a God of details, and the Bible is jam-packed with details.

It wasn't long before I became intrigued with understanding everything about God. Spoiler Alert: You will never understand everything about God, but once you delve into the Bible, the intrigue never ends. When you begin to know the true character of God, it's a lot easier to trust Him. Truth and trust walk hand in hand. I used to see everything through the lenses of a punishing God, but I started to realize God was constantly trying to steer people away from trouble and sending angels to help protect them all the time. He wasn't the one sending the trouble; He was the one ushering people out of danger and enslavement. I started to see that God repeatedly gave the people warnings and guidance, but it was the people who kept ignoring God's warnings and then getting themselves into bad situations. God wasn't such a bad guy after all.

It doesn't take a rocket scientist to put two and two together to see that knowledge of what God was saying kept people from being destroyed. That Hosea 4:6 Bible verse seemed to work. At some point in my Bible browsing, I also came across the verse, "So also will be the word that I speak—it will not fail to do what I plan for it; it will do everything I send it to do" (Isaiah 55:11 GNT). That little light bulb went off over my head again as I comprehended that all of God's words do what they say they will do. They all work! But no sooner had that epiphany hit me than doubt came into my mind. *How do I know I can trust what God says?* God was quick to answer me with another Bible verse I found in Numbers. "God is not a man, so He does not lie. He is not human, so he does not change his mind" (Numbers 23:19 NLT). Wow, God is fast on the delivery when He wants to be! I will also admit that it was a long time later when I did put two and two together, and I noticed that Satan had actually tricked Eve in the Garden of Eden with that same kind of question: "How do you know you can trust what God says?" So it would seem that believing and trusting God are primary principles in understanding who God is.

I continually came back to the same question, what did God want me to trust Him for, and what did that have to do with being still and knowing Him? That answer, like many others, comes from the omega instead of the alpha end of things. Once you know God, it's easy to trust Him. What I continued to fail miserably at was the being still part. I didn't know, and it apparently never occurred to me, was that you have to stop asking questions long enough to actually hear the answers. God does answer us if we will sit still and listen. He wants to share all kinds of things about Himself with us. Honestly, that thought just never crossed my mind. I knew God talked to people like Moses, Abraham, and Mary, but it just didn't fully register that God talks with everybody.

I am happy to report that I finally learned to listen for God. Every day for two straight years, I spent time sitting still and listening for God. You can learn a lot when you're not the one doing all the talking. The ultimate lesson I learned was that God was asking me to trust Him in everything, in every way, every day, forever. The best part is that He is one hundred percent trustworthy, and He is completely faithful to His word. If God says it, you can trust that it is true and He is faithful to fulfill whatever He has said. So now I just needed to understand the second part of God's response, "and know that I am God."

And Know That I am God

Let's do a quick review of what we already know about God. God is good. God is love. God is Jesus' father. God is honest. God is trustworthy. God is faithful. God is really not a bad guy, and since He is part of the Triune Godhead, well, He is … God. I knew there had to be more to it than that. I was beginning to understand why Moses was so frustrated with God when he first talked to him in the burning bush, and Moses asked God who He was, and God just kept replying, "I Am that I Am." Please remember that I said God responds to us, but I didn't say we always understand the answer. Sometimes we need to go on a mission to figure out what the answer means. It can be a vicious cycle.

In my search to learn more about who God was, I learned some impressive words. God is omnipotent, omniscient, omnipresent. Omnipotent means the quality of having unlimited or very great power. Omniscient means God knows everything, and omnipresent means God is present everywhere at the same time. So we can conclude that God is really smart, really strong, and He's everywhere. I also found these really wonderful qualities about God. He is patient, kind, gentle, merciful, understanding, wise, peace-loving, forgiving, and joyful, just to name a few. The Bible also tells us that He holds all things together, He created everything that was ever created, and He makes a lot of promises which He always keeps. Gosh, I'm pretty sure God has earned every Boy Scout badge there ever was. While I am obviously being flippant, the point is that God is in everything, and He is totally unlimited. He is all-powerful, all-loving, all-knowing, and He is always available. He is our all in all.

God is in everything, and He is totally unlimited.

God is also righteous, which means He is free from sin or guilt; morally upright; virtuous, honorable, ethical and has perfect holiness. God is holy! Holy is defined as exalted or worthy of complete devotion as one perfect in goodness and righteousness. Synonyms for holy include chaste, blessed, divine, faultless, glorified, hallowed, just, pure, revered, spotless, uncorrupt, undefiled, unworldly, and venerable. Clearly, God is a lot of things—a lot of really good things.

It's also important to know that since God created all things, He also established all the rules. Succinctly stated, that means God's the boss. Consequently, someday we all will have to give an account of our lives to God. In God, we live and move and have our being, which is exactly what it says in Acts 17:28 NIV. To boil all that down, I now understood that God is my everything. He is fully able to do all things and be everything that I would ever need. That is a ton of understanding and learning, but it was illuminating that not only was God asking me to believe in Him and to trust in Him, He was also now asking me to have faith in Him that He was able to get me out of the mess my life seemed to have slipped back into again.

116

Faith is the Substance

In my continuing effort to understand what God was asking of me, now I found a very interesting yet somewhat confusing Bible verse in Hebrews 11:1 KJV, "Now faith is the substance of things hoped for, the evidence of things not seen." Obviously, God is not seen, so I got that part, I think, but the "substance" of things hoped for left me scratching my head. How can something that is nebulous be of substance? That simply didn't make any sense to me. Mr. Google was kind enough to offer the definition of substance as "the real physical matter of which a person or thing consists and which has a tangible, solid presence." Some simple synonyms for substance were listed as material, matter, mass, reality, stuff, meaning. I wasn't getting anywhere fast. So I backed up a bit and decided to see what Mr. Webster had to say about faith.

Faith is defined as the strong belief in God or in the doctrines of a religion, based on spiritual comprehension rather than proof; complete trust or confidence in someone or something. Bam! There it was again, a strong belief in the doctrines of a religion. But just before I was ready to sacrifice the lamb of religion on the altar yet again, I noticed something profound. The definition of faith actually reads the strong belief in God *or* the doctrines of a religion. The definition actually held the proof of what I was finally understanding. God is not a religion. He's God! Jesus is not a religion either! He's the Son of God. Wow, talk about lights going off all over the place. There it was, blindingly bright, right there on the page. Faith is a strong belief in God.

I then noticed that Mr. Webster had also solved the rest of my comprehension issue. Faith is based on spiritual comprehension rather than proof. Clearly, my spiritual comprehension just took a giant leap forward. God was asking me to strongly believe that even though I couldn't see Him, I could completely trust Him even though I may not have tangible proof in my hand. Belief, trust, and faith, God was after it all. However, even with this new understanding, the directive still hadn't changed: "Be still and know that I am God." But how does that produce faith? I was starting to comprehend that I had a religion, but my beliefs were screwed up, and now I had a new understanding, so I needed a faith that aligned with this new comprehension. So, where do I get that?

Back to the Bible. I knew somewhere in God's book all the answers were hiding. So I started researching where faith comes from. I found out that faith is really a big thing in the Bible. I know that sounds juvenile, but everything I knew about my faith had been shaken to the core, and I needed to know how to either reclaim it or renew it entirely. When you have been raised to believe something for over fifty years, it's a hard pill to swallow to uproot it entirely. I needed my foundation put back under me again. I had such a strong need to know what was right and where I had gone wrong or been steered in the wrong direction along the way. Suffice it to say that the entire Bible is about faith, so that became overwhelming very quickly. There are dozens and dozens of Bible verses regarding faith and believing God. I'm pretty sure there are entire books that just have Bible verses regarding faith. So I tried a different methodology to search out how you garner faith and began studying the people in the Bible who were noted as men and women of faith.

Working chronologically through the Bible, there was Noah,[4] who by the way lived a really long time, believed God when God told him that there was going to be a flood and he should build this incredibly huge boat (ark) and fill it with two of everything. Mind you, Noah did not live by any huge rivers or oceans. It took Noah somewhere around a hundred years to build the ark. Really—I'm not kidding here! I have a hard time sticking with a project for more than a week or two. Combine that astounding number with the estimate that Noah was around 500 years old when he even began building the ark, and you unequivocally have a confirmed level of faith. I don't even know how you classify such a level of faith. The adjectives elude expression, and that's coming from someone who adores a thesaurus. God also promised Noah that He would never send such a flood to wipe out everything ever again, and He gave Noah the sign of a rainbow as a covenant to that promise.

Then there was Abraham.[5] God told him to pick up everything he owned and go. Just go! Not a lot of direction— just go. Amazingly enough, he did! God also told Abraham that he would be the father of all nations, and his offspring would be as numerous as the stars in the sky or the grains of sand on the beach. That's a lot of children by any measure. I'm

---

[4] "Noah" Genesis 5:32-10:1 NIV.

[5] "Abraham" Genesis 17 NIV.

119

not sure I would have wanted to believe for that many. The faith part becomes astonishing because Abraham was 100 years old at the time of this promise! Well, I guess that's young if you compare it to when Noah started his faith journey at 500 years old. Needless to say, Sarah, Abraham's wife, was pretty amused with God's sense of humor since she was 99 years old at the time. Not funny, God! But Abraham persevered, and after a number of trials and tribulations, Abraham became known as the father of the whole Hebrew nation. God had made good on the covenant promise He made Abraham so many years prior.

Moving right along, there was a young man named Joseph[6] who had a prophetic (God-inspired) dream that he was going to be sensationally rich and prosperous someday. Unfortunately for him, though, he mistakenly flaunted his prophetic promise to his bunch of super wardrobe jealous brothers that eventually plotted to kill their elegantly dressed brother. They chickened out at the last minute but decided to sell him off to a passing caravan of slave traders. (That sure sounds like such a better plan!) Joseph was enslaved for years in the house of the high-ranking Egyptian official Potiphar; then he gets accused of attacking the Pharaoh's wife and finds himself imprisoned for a whole bunch more years. Definitely not sounding like a dream come true at this point, but God steps on stage and Joseph is pulled front and center and interprets a strange prophetic dream for the Pharaoh. Turns out that the interpretation saved the nation from a seven-year famine, and the nation became the super-power of the age. In profound gratitude, Pharaoh promotes Joseph to second in command over all of the Pharaoh's

---

[6] "Joseph" Genesis 37 NIV.

120

domain. Ultimately, Joseph's dream of prosperity comes true, and his brothers humbly bow down before him, finally bringing the God-inspired promise to fruition. I decided hanging onto that dream through decades of enslavement and imprisonment warrants a faith honorable mention.

Of course, as I've mentioned several times already, God favored Moses[7] and used him mightily in His divine plans for the Hebrew nation. But Moses' story isn't all hugs and kisses either. As a matter of fact, it started off really rocky because the Pharaoh at this time was totally maniacal and had put out an edict to kill all the first-born male Hebrew children under the age of two. A horrendous slaughter of children ensued, causing Moses' mother to try and hide Moses from certain death. In God's incredible plan, Moses gets saved by the strangest twist of fate. The Pharaoh's daughter, who was childless, finds Moses in the Nile and considers him a gift from the gods, and raises him as her own son. Apparently, God really enjoys raising up His enslaved children under Pharaoh's nose. Moses is now in line for the throne of Egypt!

Jump ahead a couple of decades, and Moses kills an Egyptian who had killed a Hebrew slave. The penalty for killing an Egyptian at that time was death, so Moses fled Egypt into the desert to escape a second death threat from the Pharaoh. Moses eventually marries a Midian woman and becomes a shepherd which led to his encounter with the famous burning bush.[8] God spoke to Moses and asked him to lead His people to

---

[7] "Moses" Exodus 2 NIV. "Moses birth."

[8] "Moses" Exodus 3:1-4 NIV. "Moses at the Burning Bush."

freedom from the oppressive rule of the Egyptian Pharaoh that just happened to be his adoptive grandfather. Moses hemmed and hawed, but in the end, he did what God had asked him to do. Pharaoh, however, was not at all on board with the plan, and ten very nasty plagues ensued until he coalesced and set the Hebrew people free.

Several million, yes million, Hebrew people packed up everything they owned plus a couple of million dollars worth of Egyptian treasures and headed out of town. They trounced merrily along after a big cloud during the day and a huge pillar of fire at night until they found themselves in quite a pickle. They were smack right up against the Red Sea and Pharaoh, having come to his senses, realized he needed the slaves and set out in chariots after them. Spotlight on Moses, please. Moses had faced death down several times already, but now he was facing the certain death of millions of lives if he didn't come up with a plan. He did the only thing he could; he went to God for help with this massive life and death crisis. God gave him a very simple instruction response to his plea, "Stretch out your staff over the water Moses."[9] Dear ladies and gentlemen, I need to make something crystal clear here, his staff was a walking stick, a long piece of wood. What good could that possibly do to save millions of lives against the chariot warriors of Pharaoh?

This, my friends, is when the rubber of your faith literally meets the road. Moses had to have enough faith in God that no matter how ridiculous that instruction seemed, God was going

---

[9] Exodus 14:21 GNT "Then Moses stretched out his hand over the sea, and the Lord drove the sea back by a strong east wind all night and made the sea dry land, and the waters were divided."

to rescue them. Folks, the Red Sea was 10.5 miles across where they were standing. His staff was about five feet in length. Do the math! Now that was a stretch of faith in no uncertain terms. As you may know, God rewarded Moses' faith, and He caused the water to push back and allow the Israelites to cross over the ten-plus miles on dry land, and what's even better? God also brought the water crashing back down on Pharaoh's chariots completing and sealing the best rescue mission of all time. It's noteworthy that God had also made a covenant promise to the Israelites that He was going to give them a land flowing with milk and honey—apparently hot commodities at that time.

Our men of faith parade continues with David,[10] Jesse's eighth son. God gave David the promise when he was just a boy around 15 years old of becoming the king of Israel. The prophet Samuel anointed him, and then David was promptly sent back out into the fields to watch the flocks. It wasn't for another 15 years till David was actually crowned king. He had to slay a rather nasty Philistine giant in the meantime and was on the run from the current King Saul, who became jealous of David and was determined to kill him. Shepherding sheep and hiding out in caves on the run does not sound like the royal palace, but David clung to the promised word of God sealed with an oil-anointed covenant. He was renowned for his praise and worship of God as he sought to know God's heart more and more.

While there are many noteworthy women of faith in the Bible, I'm only going to add one here because she is the most

[10] "David" 1 Samuel 16-17 NIV.

noteworthy. That would be Jesus' mother, Mary.[11] She was a paragon of faith when you think about what she was asked to believe and accept. A messenger angel named Gabriel showed up one day and announced that God had chosen Mary to give birth to the Son of God. Furthermore, she would become impregnated by the Holy Spirit. I don't know about you, but that sounds pretty far-fetched to me. As a matter of fact, it sounds totally, completely, and utterly insane! To make matters just a tad worse, women back then were stoned to death for becoming pregnant outside of wedlock. Honestly, I find myself baffled no matter how many times I read this story knowing that Mary said okay to this plan. I am fully persuaded that by today's standards, this would have been deemed sheer lunacy. But Mary had exactly what I was trying to find. She had the very essence of faith. A faith so strong in the goodness and faithfulness of God that she trusted and believed, unwaveringly, that God would do exactly what He had said He would do—the impossible! She believed that the completely invisible Spirit of God would create in her a fully tangible substance of a child. Essentially her faith was the substance of things hoped for, and God evidenced the things not seen.

So I reasoned from all these pillars of faith[12] that faith comes from hearing God and believing Him to do the impossible in your life no matter what the circumstances look like or how long it takes to accomplish. That very realization was made plain to me in Romans 10:17, "So then faith comes by hearing,

[11] "Mary" Luke 1:26-38 NIV "The Annunciation—The Birth of Jesus Foretold"

[12] "Pillars of faith" Hebrews 11:1-40 NIV is often known as the Bible's Hall of Fame for faith.

and hearing by the word of God." I finally understood that it is not by my doing or striving or endeavoring to accomplish or even understand what God was doing but to trust Him to faithfully execute the plans He had already designed for me from the beginning of time. Not only would He give me the strength, understanding, and faith to accomplish these things, He Himself would be both the author and the finisher[13] of it all. I really did just have to be still and know that He was God.

Faith the Size of a Mustard Seed

As I have openly already attested to, I really struggled with the be still part for months, but since I was still convalescing, I spent a lot of time talking with Jesus and relentlessly asking Him questions about His plans for my life and for greater understanding of His truth. Early one evening in fall, the flowers in my back porch planters were looking pretty much dead, but I told Jesus I wasn't ready for them to be dead. I hated to give up how beautiful the planters had been all summer. Jesus surprised me by telling me to pray over them to come back. He told me to lay my hands on each planter and pray for them to return. I confess that my level of faith was not yet that stellar, but I obediently laid my hands on each planter and prayed a simple prayer over each of them. I told Jesus I was also worried about one of the trees in front of my house that I feared was going to die. Most of the leaves had fallen off even

---

[13] "Looking on Jesus, the author and finisher of faith, who having joy set before him, endured the cross, despising the shame, and now sitteth on the right hand of the throne of God." Hebrews 12:2 Douay-Rheims Bible

before the cold weather had fully set in, and there were only a few dried-up leaves still hanging on. I asked Jesus if I should pray over that tree too, and He said I should; I obediently did.

My trusted readers, we have only been together on this book journey for a couple of chapters, but I need you to understand the magnitude of what I'm about to tell you. Sometimes faith takes a gargantuan leap forward. After I prayed over my flowers and tree, I completely forgot about them and went inside. I really didn't have much expectation that they would somehow instantly spring back to life right before my eyes. I'm being honest here. But the following morning when I went on my back porch to enjoy my morning cup of tea, I was flabbergasted to see that all three of my planters were bursting with new plants shooting up through the soil! Hundreds of new shoots were poking their heads up. I could not believe my eyes! I stood in total shock and awe. God had indeed heard my prayers and blessed my plants to return. I need you to hear me—hundreds and hundreds of tiny little new plants were sprouting up! My faith soared like an Apollo rocket. Suddenly it occurred to me that I had prayed over the tree out front as well. I hobbled as fast as my legs could take me through the house to check the tree out front. (Pregnant pause for added drama.)

Praise God! Hallelujah! The sickly tree had sprouted hundreds of new baby leaves all over the entire tree! I was dumbfounded and ecstatic all at the same time. How was this possible? Were my eyes deceiving me? What in the world were my neighbors going to think? The God of the impossible proved His word of faithfulness to me. I was seeing the very manifestation of the Bible verse Luke 17:6 NIV "The apostles said to the Lord, 'Increase our faith!' He replied, "If you have faith as small as a mustard seed[14], you can say to this mulberry tree, 'Be uprooted and planted in the sea,' and it will obey you." I had prayed a simple prayer with the scarcest of faith to see anything happen and God faithfully and miraculously brought life back to my flowers and tree (albeit not a mulberry tree). God is the God of the impossible. God increased my faith a hundred-fold that day. I'm not exactly sure how the changes in those flowers and that tree would be classified. I don't know if they were miracles, signs, wonders, or raising the dead, but they were real, and no one but no one could ever make me doubt God's word or power again. I was now the proud owner of all the faith I could hold.

---

[14] "Mustard seeds" are the small round seeds of various mustard plants. The seeds are usually about 1 to 2 millimetres (0.039 to 0.079 in) in diameter and may be colored from yellowish white to black. Retrieved from: https://en.wikipedia.org/wiki/Mustard_seed. Accessed 24 August 2021.

God is the God of the impossible.

Chapter 5

When Life
Springs Back

Renewed Hope

Those miracles are when the Bible finally became real to me. The healing miracles made me aware that there was something greater than me at work here, but the flower and tree miracles were a game-changer for me. They had nothing to do with my potential for the hypothetical nine lives or it just not being my time yet. They were pure, unadulterated, coming back to life almost literally before my eyes, miracles. I guess some of us are harder to impress than others. I don't think I realized just how hard-headed I actually was until this very moment. Seeing is believing!

Astonishment, crazy joy, staggering amazement captivated me as I just kept looking and touching those new shoots to plaster in my mind that they were real and not just an overactive imagination. Now not only did I have belief, trust, and faith, but I had a renewed sense of hope. I believed that God was truly going to restore my life and uphold all the promises He made me that first day on the balcony. Hope is a beautiful thing. My spirit was now just like the baby shoots, new and springing back to life. Abounding in joy was something completely foreign to me after everything that had happened to me. Abounding is a really good thing! Life renewed is what God is all about. He brings things to life and back to life. Suddenly I was a living testimony, and I wanted everyone to know about it.

The Bible verse rang in my ears over and over, "Faith is the substance of things hoped for." It was now conspicuously evident that faith and hope go hand in hand. It seems you simply can't have one without the other. You can't have faith for something when you have no hope, and you can't have hope when you have no faith that the thing can actually happen. When you have been imprisoned in fear, anger, frustration, disbelief, guilt, shame, desolation, pain, or any such feeling for such a long time that it can seem impossible to hope for anything to break through and change your circumstances, but I am living proof that God can, does and will do that for you too. This book is about instilling a new hope in you for something you may currently believe is impossible. I'm here to tell you that God is in the impossible business, and He is open for business 24 hours a day, 7 days a week. Please step this way.

You may be saying to yourself right about now that you tried to believe for things before just to be disappointed, and you simply don't have the strength to hope again, but as long as you are still drawing breath, then God's not done with you yet. May I remind you of my "Crashed and Burned" section of this book? I was as low as low could get. I was the epitome of hopelessness at that point in my life. I certainly could not see how God was ever going to make anything good happen in my life, but He did. I encourage you to borrow some of my faith and hope to sustain you for a bit longer as you continue to read because I still have more miracles to tell you about and the miracles I firmly believe are still to come in your life too.

Hope is a powerful thing. Never underestimate someone with hope. They will scale tall mountains and ford rushing streams for what they hope to achieve. I recently watched a television series about homesteaders in Alaska. Those folks are what legends are made of. They withstood colossal odds for the hope of securing free land. If they built a home and lived in it for five years, the 160 acres of land that they staked out would be deeded to them. They faced absolutely barbaric weather and living conditions as well as food, water, and heat shortage challenges that I cannot even fathom facing. But that hope of owning their own land drove them to overcome every hair-raising obstacle that Mother Nature threw at them. And can she be nasty! No matter, they simply did not let defeat enter into their vocabulary, let alone their minds.

They reminded me of what the Israelites must have been like. They had the promise of their own land; if they believed God and made it across the life-threatening desert conditions, they would inherit it free of charge. Full-blown regions and territories would be handed over to them if they could hold onto the hope of their faith and the faithfulness of their God. But like most of us, they wavered—a lot. Unlike Mother Nature, God gave them food, water, and shelter but holding onto their faith and hope was a daily trial. Some days they were better than others but being ensconced as an overcomer was a slippery slope for sure.

What are you hoping for that you think is impossible? What dreams have you pushed way down in your spirit for fear of them never coming true? When was the last time you even allowed yourself to hope or dream for something? When was the last time you saw a miracle? If it's been a while, may I remind you that faith and hope go hand in hand? Matthew 9:29 KJV specifically tells us, "According to your faith, be it done unto you." I encourage you to find your tiny mustard seed of faith and start hoping and believing again. You need to have some tiny measure of expectation to see something happen. God loves a challenge, and He is anxiously waiting to show you just how amazingly He can change your life.

Covenants

You will recall from the last chapter some of our Bible champions of faith. God made crazy promises to them, and through thick and thin, they held fast to those promises because when God makes a promise, He covenants with you. So what's the big deal with a covenant over a promise? God never breaks His covenants. We as humans break our promises all the time, but God never

does. A covenant is a binding promise between individuals, groups, or nations to do or not do something. Unlike contracts that can be annulled or amended, covenants stand firm from generation to generation, and God never forgets or reneges on His portion of the agreement. He is faithful to fulfill every word of it, so you can trust Him 100 percent of the time. So go ahead, start believing, trusting, hoping, and dreaming again.

We've already discussed the covenants God made with Noah, Abraham, Moses, and David, but there were a couple of other big-time covenants worth mentioning too. Namely, the very first covenant God made with mankind, Adam and Eve to be specific, and the last one that He made with Jesus, known as the New or Everlasting Covenant. Not coincidentally, these two covenants are actually tied together for all eternity; the first and the last, the Alpha and the Omega. While covenants are not to be broken, they do contain if/then components. God says *if* you do this part, *then* I will do this part. It is an agreement between two entities to each uphold their portion of the deal. God's original covenant with mankind, Adam and Eve, was for eternal life as long as they did not eat of the Tree of the Knowledge of Good and Evil.[1] Man's part of the deal was to avoid eating of the tree and avoid having the knowledge of evil. They already had the knowledge of good because they were living with God, who is all good. Unfortunately, Adam and Eve chose to renege on their part of the deal and enter into the knowledge of evil and immediately upon eating that fruit broke their covenant promise with God.

---

[1] "... but of the tree of the knowledge of good and evil you shall not eat, for in the day that you eat of it you shall surely die." Genesis 2:17 NKJV.

The bad news is that evil is the opposite of good, so instead of eternal life, it creates eternal death. God had to create both good and evil if mankind was to have a free will choice, otherwise, we would all just be slaves to God and not children. God gave mankind full dominion over the earth and all therein. We wanted for nothing. God also gave us the warning about life and death to protect us. I'm pretty sure that if someone gave me a bottle of poison and explicitly told me that if I drink it, it's going to kill me, I would not drink it, but the enemy of our souls is a cunning liar, and he tempted Adam and Eve with his crafty lies. Millennials later, he's still doing it. Satan continually tempts us to go against or rebel against God's will. The scripture John 10:10 KJV reminds us over and over that the thief (Satan) only comes to steal, kill and destroy us but thank God there is another part to that verse. It's Jesus' promise to us, "But I have come that they may have life and have it abundantly."

Perhaps one of the most famous and well-known of all Bible verses is John 3:16 NLT, "For this is how God loved the world: He gave His one and only Son so that everyone who believes in Him will not perish but have eternal life." That, my friends, is the Good News of Jesus Christ! God sent His Son, Jesus, to redeem us from that original fateful decision of seeking the knowledge of evil. God still wants to uphold His part of the original covenant He made with us, so He made a way for us back into eternal life with Him. We get a "do-over!" We get to choose God in the person of Jesus Christ over evil and death. He truly is the God of second chances.

I don't know about you, but I am equally sure that if someone told me that I could have a do-over for an especially bad decision, I'd be very interested to know-how. So here's how: Choose Christ! Which is essentially making a free will choice for God all over again. Because covenants remain intact from generation to generation, and you are part of mankind, you can choose to reject evil and be rejoined to God's original promise of eternal life through the New and Everlasting Covenant God is offering us. And that is known as grace—the unmerited mercy and favor of God.

Grace

So you may be wondering how this whole do-over grace[2] process works. You may recall earlier in this book, I mentioned that Jesus paid the price for us—the us being Adam, Eve, and all the rest of mankind. I also mentioned that Jesus bought us our fast pass ticket to eternal life, but that still doesn't explain the process. I'm going to try and make this as simple an explanation as I can, but please know in no uncertain terms it is the most important information that you could ever receive; your eternal life literally depends on it.

Ephesians 2:8 ESV tells us that by grace, we have been saved through faith. And this is not our own doing; it is the gift of God. God gave us a gift. The gift was actually His Son Jesus Christ coming down to earth in the form of a man to redeem

---

[2] "Grace" in Christianity is the free and unmerited favour of God as manifested in the salvation of sinners and the bestowing of blessings. Common Christian teaching is that grace is unmerited mercy (favor) that God gave to humanity by sending His Son, Jesus Christ, to die on a cross, thus securing man's eternal salvation from sin. Retrieved from: https://en.wikipedia.org/wiki/Divine_grace. Accessed 3 July 2021.

mankind's breach of the original covenant with God. We know that Adam and Eve botched things up when they were tempted and deceived by the consummate evil, the devil, which equated to breaking their portion of the covenant. This rebellion against the one covenant stipulation God had for them resulted in them forfeiting eternal life. The penalty they agreed to was that they would eventually die if they broke their covenant promise with God. The initial breaking of this first covenant is known as original sin. Adam and Eve were banished from Eden to spend the rest of their lives toiling on earth.

God continued through centuries of time to re-covenant with us again and again but being human, we kept falling short of the glory set before us, so in Ephesians 2:4-5 ESV we read, "But God, being rich in mercy,[3] because of the great love with which he loved us, even when we were dead in our trespasses, made us alive together with Christ—by grace you have been saved." Romans 5:8 ESV says it even more succinctly, "But God shows His love for us in that while we were still sinners, Christ died for us." We are saved by grace, and Jesus is that grace bearer. Jesus established the New and Everlasting Covenant guaranteeing us eternal life. How, you may ask?

Here is a super-condensed essence of everything that the Old Testament and New Testament points us towards to gain our eternal lives back again. God realized that in our frail humanness, we could not uphold our end of the covenant, so

---

[3] "Mercy" can be defined as "compassion or forbearance shown especially to an offender or to one subject to one's power"; and also "a blessing that is an act of divine favor or compassion. To be at someone's mercy" indicates a person being "without defense against someone." Retrieved from: https://en.wikipedia.org/wiki/Mercy Accessed 3 July 2021.

He had to work out another way for us to secure our eternal lives with Him. Since He is a Triune God, three parts in one, He sent the Son portion of Himself, Jesus, to earth to fulfill our end of the covenant once and for all. You will remember from our earlier discussion about the covenant God made with Mary that she would be overshadowed by the

> We could never hold up our end of the covenant, so God sent Jesus to fulfill our part of the covenant once and for all

Holy Spirit and conceive Jesus, pure and without sin. By that miracle, Jesus became fully man and He could now make a covenant with God the Father as a representative of mankind. But also being fully God and perfect in every way, He would be able to uphold the covenant forever.

The laws that God had given to the Israelites through Moses stipulated that once a year they could atone for their sins and rebellions against God by placing their sins metaphorically upon a spotless lamb and then sacrificing it to God. The blood of the lamb represented that God's people desired to be reconciled back to God once again. The problem was that they kept slipping up and not upholding their end of the covenant year after year. Enter in Jesus. Jesus, being fully man and fully God but without any sin, was now able to perfectly uphold mankind's portion of the original covenant promise between God and man. However, 2000 years ago, to fulfill the atonement requirement thereby upholding all the Hebrew laws that God had established with His people, a blood sacrifice had to be offered.

Jesus being perfectly pure and without sin, allowed His life to be slain to be that blood sacrifice for all mankind. Jesus

Jesus shed blood fulfilled every requirement of the law for man to be reconciled back to God

died a brutal death crucified on a cross taking upon Himself all of mankind's sins just as the lambs had done for centuries before. His shed blood fulfilled every requirement of the law for man to be reconciled back to God. But God, knowing our human weakness, offered us an even more phenomenal new covenant opportunity. Jesus could be our eternal atonement. Because Jesus was both man and God, He is able to continue without sin, thus upholding the covenant for all eternity.

God the Father performed the greatest miracle of all time to make this offer possible. He raised Jesus from the dead as a man and brought Him back into heaven as fully man and fully God to live forever. This new covenant had "if this—then that" parts to it as all covenants do. God said, "If you will believe that my son, Jesus, came down from heaven, became a man, died for the atonement of your sins (once and for all), was resurrected back to life and ascended back to heaven, then I will promise you eternal life. Essentially, if you will believe Me, trust Me and have faith in all that Jesus Christ has done, then I will do what I promised: you will have eternal life in heaven with Me. Jesus' sacrifice and God's loving mercy and grace offer us the free gift of eternal salvation. It is your fast pass, paid in full, eternal do-over. This is not only the Good News of Jesus Christ but the best news you could ever know!

Choosing Christ

So here it is, the offer in writing to receive the New Covenant promise of Jesus Christ. I encourage you with every fiber of my body to receive the salvation of Jesus Christ for yourself. Simply pray this prayer with me now.

"Father God, I'm sorry for all the times I have freely chosen to do things that go against You, and I want to change that now. I do believe that Your son, Jesus, came down from heaven, became a man, died for the atonement of my sins, was resurrected back to life and ascended to heaven and is seated with You there. I ask Jesus now to be my Savior and rule over my life forevermore. Amen."

Congratulations if you just prayed that prayer! I welcome you into the family of God. You have just made the greatest, grandest, most gigantic, tremendous, enormous, excellent, glorious, amazing, exceptional, fabulous, smart, stupendous, and incredible all-around decision of your life! Praise God! Hallelujah! You surely do not yet understand the magnitude of that prayer and the promise it holds. But I can assure you that your life will never be the same from this moment forward because the Creator and Ruler of all the universe is now the champion of your life. The definition of a champion is one that does battle for another's rights or honor; a militant advocate or defender; one who shows marked superiority; first place. Synonyms for champion include unparalleled, victor, vanquisher, vindicator, warrior, upholder, guardian, defeater, supporter, undefeated, the greatest. I include such a lengthy list to help impress upon you just what a big deal having Jesus as your Savior champion really means.

Heirs

In Romans 5:17 ESV, we read, "For if, because of one man's trespass, death reigned through that one man, much more will those who receive the abundance of grace and the free gift of righteousness reign in life through the one man Jesus Christ." Again in Titus 3:7 ESV, we see a similar assertion, "So that being justified by His grace we might become heirs according to the hope of eternal life." You may be saying to yourself, "So what does that all mean and have to do with Jesus being a champion?" Well, let me expound upon all of that. Because of one man's trespass, death reigned refers to Adam's original sin, which carried with it the penalty of death for all of mankind for rebelling against God's will. But the remainder of that verse assures us that because of God's ultimate and undying mercy towards us, He gave us the free gift of grace through Jesus Christ, thereby restoring us to eternal life. You may have also noticed the word reign in both of those scriptures, and with good reason.

Reign means to rule, have power over, have dominion, or prevail, none of which seem to have anything to do with grace, hope, or covenant. It does, however, have a lot to do with being a champion. When God resurrected Jesus from the dead, death being what evil produces, death was defeated, removed, and vanquished. Jesus overcame and vindicated mankind from the sin rebellion of Adam and Eve, and the penalty was expunged. We fully belonged to God again, and all the covenant promises He had made with us over the centuries. We were given our dominion over the earth back again.

Because of Jesus' great sacrifice for us, God the Father gave Jesus all power and authority over heaven, and everyone who believes in Him is given their gift of eternal life back again. But there's more! You will recall that Ephesians 2:5 ESV told us that we were saved by grace; however, the scripture continues in Ephesians 2:6 ESV and goes on to say, "And God raised us up with Christ and seated us with Him in the heavenly realms in Christ Jesus." *What?! How in the world is that possible?* Well, that's the catch. It's not in the world; it's in the spirit. Recall you are made in God's image, so you are three in one as well: spirit, soul, and body. When you accept Christ as your Lord and Savior and make the profession of faith, God raises your spirit to sit with Jesus in heaven. And there's even more!

Once Jesus was resurrected from the dead, He returned to earth for forty days. He spent time with His disciples, and just before His ascension back into heaven, Jesus did something incredible. He gave His disciples authority over all the power of the enemy (Luke 10:19)[4], and He gave them "the keys of the kingdom of heaven so that whatever you bind on earth will be bound in heaven, and whatever you loose on earth will be loosed in heaven" (Matthew 16:19).[5] Essentially Jesus gave His believing disciples (which, as believers, you and I are included) spiritual authority both here on earth and in heaven. Astonishingly, He wasn't done yet! He also "made you a king

---

[4] Luke 10:19 NKJV "Behold, I give you the authority to trample on serpents and scorpions, and over all the power of the enemy, and nothing shall by any means hurt you."

[5] Matthew 16:19 ESV "I will give you the keys of the kingdom of heaven, and whatever you bind on earth shall be bound in heaven, and whatever you loose on earth shall be loosed in heaven."

and a priest unto God" (Revelation 1:6).[6] Thus we rule and reign with Jesus both here and now and in the spiritual realm. Are you starting to see why having Jesus as your champion is such an extraordinary thing? I sure hope so.

Likewise, I hope you are now seeing the correlation of grace, hope, and covenant as well. Let me sum all of that up. Due totally to God's mercy and grace, we were given the hope of eternal life again, and because of Jesus' sacrifice for mankind, our covenant relationship with God was reinstated forevermore to rule and reign as co-heirs with Christ Jesus. Well, I'm betting that your head is spinning like a top by now. That's a lot to digest and sounds a lot like religion, but I remind you that God is not a religion, He's our Creator, and He has plans for each one of us. Jesus' sacrifice bought each believer freedom from eternal death. But why? Just what are these plans of God's for each of us, and how do we figure them out?

If I was to spout off to you religiously, I would just quote 2 Timothy 1:9 ESV, "Who saved us and called us to a holy calling, not because of our works but because of His own purpose and grace, which He gave us in Christ Jesus before the ages began" or Titus 2:11-12 ESV, "For the grace of God has appeared, bringing salvation for all people, training us to renounce ungodliness and worldly passions and to live self-controlled, upright, and godly lives in the present age" but that probably wouldn't help you much to understand the plans God has for you as an individual. You would be left with more

---

[6] Revelation 1:5-6 BSB "and from Jesus Christ, the faithful witness, the firstborn from the dead, and the ruler of the kings of the earth. To Him who loves us and has released us from our sins by His blood, who has made us to be a kingdom, priests to His God and Father—to Him be the glory and power forever and ever! Amen."

questions than answers. What is a holy calling? What is God's purpose for me in this present age? What exactly is a present age anyway? This, of course, then begs the question, "How do we then proceed?"

I suggest we back up just a bit to the part where Jesus is our champion. The part where He does battle for your rights, advocates, defends, vanquishes, guards, and supports you. Since we were made in His image, God wants us to help others do the same thing Jesus did for us. He wants us to step into a champion role to do battle for others' rights. He wants us to advocate for our friends, family, co-workers, and everyone who needs defending and salvation. Why? Because Jesus bought that fast pass, free do-over, for every single person. Once we freely receive it, we get to let everybody else in on the deal, and what a deal it is, but I'm getting a little ahead of myself here. You're still trying to figure out what your champion role looks like. So how do we do that?

Doctor, Lawyer, or Indian Chief

Now that you are armed with a bit more knowledge, let's consider what your champion role options might look like. What's your role? Were you meant to be a mom or a missionary? How about a doctor, lawyer, or Indian chief? (Stay calm, no social statement intended.) What about an entertainer or musician? Maybe a priest, prophet, or king? (It could happen!) Maybe you house the cure for cancer, multiple sclerosis, or auto-immune disease. Possibly you are the next Olympic champion, Master's golf champion, or the Kentucky Derby's

> *God has created and equipped you perfectly for the destiny He has in mind for you*

winning jockey. Well, somebody has to be, why not you? The point is that God has created and equipped you perfectly for the destiny He has in mind for you. Now you just have to step into it. Gosh, it seems we are right back to the beginning of where are you and where do you want to go?

Exactly! But now you are armed with something you didn't have before—directions! God actually wrote your destiny right into your DNA, plus He gave you the consummate how-to book for living into the fullness of that destiny, the Bible. The very things you love to do, think about doing someday, or have always wondered what it would be like to do, are the very things God has placed in your heart and mind to do. Your life circumstances may have steered you in a very different direction, but now you are behind the wheel, and you can choose to change lanes, directions, or your ultimate destination because when God is for you, no one can be against you. (Romans 8:31 BSB)[7] God always makes a way. As a matter of fact, He has already gone ahead of you and made the way clear.[8] And don't forget you have a fast pass to the front of the line. So now let's get to seriously thinking about where you want to go or who you want to be.

The options may seem limitless, and to some extent, that would be true, but don't let that inhibit or scare you from

---

[7] Romans 8:31 BSB "What then shall we say in response to these things? If God is for us, who can be against us?"

[8] John 14:3 NLT "When everything is ready, I will come and get you, so that you will always be with me where I am."

narrowing down the possible selections that would truly make your heart sing. Here is another Spoiler Alert: You are the only one stopping you from doing exactly what you want to do! Let your mind run wild for a little bit and see what ideas surface in all that gray matter in your head. This may take longer for some of you than others because you haven't allowed yourself this kind of freedom for a long time, if ever. I was 52 years old before I ever truly thought about what I wanted to do with my life or, for that matter, what I even liked or what it might take to accomplish it.

Eventually, it occurred to me that I might want to ask God what He was thinking I should do when He made me. He encouraged me to search my heart and that I would find the answers there. Armed with my semi-automatic question BB gun again, I besieged God with dozens of questions. What about this or this or this ... seldom waiting for His answer but anxious to figure it all out. What I eventually remembered was I needed to search my heart for what passionately moved me every time I thought of it. Being passionately moved is very different from something just being interesting or appealing to you. Being passionate about something makes you move and take action. No one ever won an Olympic medal because they thought it would be nice to stand on one of those medal platforms. No one ever ran a 5K race because they thought it would be fun to be the person who broke the finish line ribbon. Thomas Edison would not have tried 3,000 different theories to invent the lightbulb if he wasn't passionate about it. Walt Disney wouldn't have gone bankrupt three times before he created Disneyland if he wasn't passionate about it. Elvis

Presley would never have achieved 101 gold records after he was fired from the Grand Ole Opry if he wasn't passionate about singing.

While I'm not advocating for bankruptcy, what are you that passionate about? Remember you have unbridled your heart and, hopefully, your imagination to romp freely through the canyons of your mind. Boldly going where you may never have trodden before. Depending on your age, experience, ambition, or risk aversion, your answers will vary greatly. Depending on the fire, or lack of it, in your belly, your answers will be vastly different. Depending on how far you have gone off course from your life's true destiny, your answers will bear no resemblance to each other, but that's perfectly fine; as a matter of fact, the more diverse, the better because God made you unique, and so is your destiny.

Here's a little clue to help you analyze which possibility is really holding all your potential in it. It's the one God has actually been preparing you for all your life. All your training, schooling, jobs, life experience, talent, likes and dislikes, love, and even failures have in one way or another all contributed to equipping you for this moment in your life. There's an axiom that says, "God doesn't call the equipped, He equips the called." God was equipping you with all the skills you would need to accomplish all the plans He has for your life before you ever noticed it. Hence there is a "call" on your life. Before you go getting all nervous on me, there's a call on everyone's life; some are just bigger than others by comparison. Must be why God warned us to avoid comparing ourselves to one another. Your call is custom-made just for you.

So what exactly does a call on your life mean? It means that God created a very specific destiny for you to fulfill in your life that will bring Him glory. Many people refer to this as their purpose in life, but it's more than that. It's the fulfillment of God's plans for you. There's Jeremiah 29:11 NIV again, "'For I know the plans I have for you,' declares the LORD, 'plans to prosper you and not to harm you, to give you a future and a hope.'" From that verse, we can also deduce that His plans are both good and hopeful which is very beneficial to know. There are multiple places throughout the Bible that give some basic overall instructions for mankind's purpose. Jesus told us, "You shall love the Lord your God with all your heart and with all your soul and with all your might (Deuteronomy 6:5 ESV)." The prophet Micah tells us, "He has told you, O man, what is good; and what does the Lord require of you but to do justice, and to love kindness, and to walk humbly with your God?" (Micah 6:8 ESV). Solomon sums things up rather succinctly, saying, "The end of the matter; all has been heard. Fear [respect] God and keep His commandments, for this is the whole duty of man" (Ecclesiastes 12:13 ESV).

Sphere of Influence

But that age-old question may still haunt us, "What is my call and my purpose?" To glean that answer, we need to analyze the hopes and dreams that are hidden in your heart and may have started to surface once you let your mind wander freely. Make a list of the ideas and thoughts that popped into your head when you gave your heart and mind free rein. Here are some good questions to help you think about the things that really matter to you. What areas of interest have always intrigued you or have you been drawn towards? What areas have the exact opposite effect on you? What things have always come easily to you? What especially unique talents do you possess? What industries appeal to you? What makes you smile *every* time you think of it? What things 'get your goat' so to speak? What societal things infuriate you? If you could go anywhere in the world, where would you go and why? Are you outgoing or shy? Are you a leader or a follower? Are you driven or laid back? Are you content or ambitious? Are you analytical or artistic? Do you like working with kids, adults, the elderly, or the handicapped? Are you a team player, or do you like to go it alone? Are you adventurous or cautious? Do you see the sunny side of things, or are you more apt to see the problems arise? Gee, this is starting to sound like a dating site profile, and well, it kind of is.

All of these questions help you to see what God has built into you and what areas of interest you are likely well-suited for. It helps you to think about who you are more deeply and where your limitations or natural proclivities lie. But there is more to it than that as well because a purpose or call is not a vocation, job or interest. It is the thing you are most perfectly suited to accomplish in your life and will fulfill the very ache within your bones. When you discover what that really is or looks like, you literally come alive. Your days aren't long enough to contain all the joy and excitement these activities bring with them. If you extrapolate this verse, you will see how it rings completely true. Romans 14:17 GNT explains, "For God's kingdom does not consist of food and drink, but of righteousness, peace, and joy produced by the Holy Spirit."

When we are rightly aligned (righteousness) with God's (Holy Spirit) heavenly purpose, we will find ourselves living in a state of peace (fulfillment) and joy (perpetual happiness). God wants each of us to live in a perpetual state of happiness, fulfillment, and blessing. So when He created us, He built all the desires into us to accomplish that. If, however, you are saying, "I'm not feeling that way" that would be a perfect clue that you are not yet moving in your God-given purpose. But as you truly search the deep things of your heart and soul, you will unearth the things that can lead you into that stage of your life, and then you will see just how amazingly God has prepared you for it. Keep in mind that you may not yet have reached the age where that becomes apparent. You may not know that your niche in life even exists yet. I had never considered my godly life's purpose until I was 52 years old. Hmm … just now realizing that a lot of lights went off for me when I was 52. Until that time, I thought the only way you could really devote your life to God was to be a priest or a nun. Laity didn't count as being fully committed, and being a missionary seemed way out of the realm of possibilities for me; being an author never even crossed my mind.

As a matter of fact, working in the marketplace, media, school, arts and entertainment, or anything outside the church for that matter didn't seem to merit the coveted title of being fully committed to God. I don't know if that thinking was a product of my upbringing or my understanding of what service to God could entail and still count as a fulfilled godly purpose.

Today's options are truly endless and come in every walk of life. This, however, created a conundrum for me. I needed to reckon with my life purpose and God's purpose for my life. Were they one-in-the-same? I had to come to the understanding that my day-to-day life wasn't my purpose; rather, I had to bring my day-to-day life into proper alignment with God, and then I would find the oh-so-elusive joy and peace that my spirit so desperately desired. I could do whatever things fulfilled my heart, but I had to do them for God's glory. That's a pretty big lesson. Far easier typed than learned.

Each of us has a purpose that God has designed us to carry out in our sphere of influence. Your sphere of influence includes your home, job, office, church, and community. If you are employed by the state or federal government, then it extends to the state, national, or perhaps even the international level too. Simply put, whoever you come in contact with is your sphere of influence. Here's an easy scripture to remember what you are supposed to be doing, "Whatever you do, do it enthusiastically, as something done for the Lord and not for men, knowing that you will receive the reward of an inheritance from the Lord. You serve the Lord Christ" (Colossians 3:23-24 HCSB). As a Christian, everywhere you go, you are taking Christ with you and modeling Him to the world; your world, your family, your friends, your co-workers, your church fellow worshippers, your neighbors, and all those you encounter along the way.

Doing it enthusiastically can only happen when you are passionate about what you are doing. Fortunately, you are most passionate about the things God has knit into your DNA before you were ever born. So as you do all the things enthusiastically both for God and for others, you are fulfilling exactly what Jesus told us were the greatest of the commandments, "Love the Lord your God with all your heart, with all your soul, and with all your mind. The second is exactly like it: You must love your neighbor as yourself" (Matthew 22:37, 39 ISV). The added bonus is that we reap true and sustained joy and fulfillment in doing so. Now that's what I call a win-win! However, there is a small caveat that I should probably mention right about now: It's not about you.

It's Not About You

"What do you mean, it's not about me?" Hey, I asked the exact same thing when God told me that too. *You mean I spent all this time trying to figure out what I'm really and truly passionate about, and now you're telling me that it's not about me? What gives?* Exactly! When we give of ourselves fully and freely loving God and others, then we glorify God and that's what it's all about. Every breath we take is to glorify God. Every good deed, every random act of kindness, every invention, every song, every reassuring word, every report, every sermon, every book written, every race run, every mountain scaled, every river forded, every everything is for God's glory. In our self-centered society, this does not sit very well with most of us. We are very accustomed to self-satisfaction, self-enlightenment, self-success, and self-fulfillment, but we don't talk about God's glory much anymore these days. That, however, is what God created us to do first and foremost. When we as models of

Christ's love, care, create, forgive, worship, and be our very best selves, we glorify God. *Taa-daa!*

Hopefully, you're still with me here because it's about to get fun. You may be wondering what exactly fun means to me, but that's not as important as what it means to Jesus. Jesus thought turning water into wine[9] was fun. He thought multiplying a couple of loaves of bread and dried-up fish to feed five thousand people[10] was fun. Jesus thought walking on water[11] was a ton of fun. He loved healing people when He wasn't even trying to or watching the leper's[12] skin transform right before the apostles' eyes. Jesus really smiled from His heart when Lazarus[13] came out of his grave and gave his sisters a big hug. Now that's what I call life springing back! That's right—miracles, signs, and wonders are Jesus' idea of fun and, well, frankly, mine too. And to take it even higher, Jesus promised us that we would do all those things and greater still. Greater still! How is that even possible? Can't tell you how many times I've asked myself that same question, but we walk in the assurance of everything God has said and Luke 1:37 ESV confirms that with God, nothing will be impossible.

So what's the catch? Simply put, it's all about God. When Jesus was ministering to the crowds that had gathered to witness His miracles, signs, and wonders, He always looked to His

---

[9] John 2:1-11 NIV "Jesus Changes Water into Wine."

[10] John 6:1-14 NIV "Jesus Feeds The Five Thousand."

[11] Matthew 14:22-33 NIV "Jesus Walks on the Water."

[12] Matthew 8 NIV "Jesus Heals a Man with Leprosy."

[13] John 11:38-44 NIV "Jesus Raises Lazarus From the Dead."

Father in heaven to see what He was doing or saying, and then He did precisely that and then thanked God for the miracles that took place. When we walk in Jesus' same immeasurable love and compassion, we will be compelled to love the same way and give our testimonies to what He has done in our lives and those around us. It is our testimony, the words of truth that come from our mouths, that give thanks and glory to God. When everything we do we attribute to God, we glorify Him, and that's our life's purpose, plain and simple—giving glory to God in the highest.

Just in case you are still not convinced, don't worry; Jesus' disciples weren't too sure about the whole miracle-working business either. After all, they did see Him crucified and die on the cross, and that definitely was not reassuring whatsoever. Of course, Jesus terrified them when He returned to them after God had resurrected[14] Him, but just before Jesus ascended[15] back into heaven, He explained to His disciples that God was going to send them a Helper[16] to figure all this miracle-working stuff out, and they should wait for the Holy Spirit. *The holy what?*

---

[14] Acts 1:1-5 BSB "Prologue to the Ascension of Jesus."

[15] Acts 1:6-11 NLT "The Ascension of Jesus."

[16] "The Helper will come—the Spirit, who reveals the truth about God and who comes from the Father. I will send Him to you from the Father, and He will speak about me." John 15:26 GNT.

When everything we do we attribute to God,
we glorify Him, and that's our life's purpose, plain
and simple—giving glory to God in the highest.

Chapter 6

All the Glory

Wait for the Holy Spirit

I really do pity the poor old apostles; they had no clue what was going on. Jesus was always throwing them some kind of curveball. As soon as they thought they understood what Jesus was up to, He'd change things up. Certainly they were not expecting to see Him crucified and they were totally and completely blown away when He returned to them raised from the dead. And while they were still scratching their heads, He goes and floats back up into heaven. Now what? Alone again! Who in the world was this new dude called the Holy Spirit something? What was His deal? They were just getting used to Jesus and all His quirky ways and habits. Now they were back to square one, and not only were the Romans terrorizing them, but the Jews were looking to kill anyone associated with Jesus too. So back into hiding they went and hoped the new guy would find them and straighten this whole mess out.

It wasn't long until the new guy blew into town, literally! The Holy Spirit showed up in Hollywood cinematic style. What the apostles failed to remember was that Jesus also said the Helper would come and imbue them with power. The dunamis[1] power of God that is. The very same power that He not only imbued Jesus with but the same power that created the entire universe and everything in it. Now that's what I'm talking about. The power that sends demons running, lepers dancing, and dead men walking. The "all mighty" power of God with which nothing shall be impossible! This Helper packed a punch.

When the Holy Spirit roared into town, no one knew what was happening, but it got everyone's attention. The very breath of God had blown into Jerusalem. The breath that when He spoke the earth, stars, oceans, and mountains came into being. As a matter of fact, everything that had ever been created was created from this very same breath. The same breath that had first been breathed into Adam and brought the entirety of humanity into being. The breath that created all things was now being breathed over the apostles, and all those gathered with them that day. It lit a fire in them that would never be extinguished. It burned a desire into their bones that burns still today, two thousand years later. That, my devoted readers, is the same power that lives inside every single believer who has made Jesus the Lord over their lives. That is the power that ensures we can do all the miracles, signs, and wonders that

---

[1] "Dunamis" The Greek word dunamis in Scripture means power, force, or ability. We derive our English word dynamite and dynamic from the Greek word dunamis. Retrieved from: https://www.christianity.com/wiki/christian-terms/what-is-the-meaning-of-dunamis-in-the-bible.html. Accessed on 5 June 2021.

Jesus did and greater still. The very breath of God is what you breathe with every breath you take. Selah!

The glory of God not only rested upon them but entered into their spirits and stirred their hearts beyond all reasoning. It is recorded that the Holy Spirit sounded like a roaring wind when it came on Pentecost, and it surely brought with it the fearlessness of a roaring lion. The Lion of Judah[2] was roaring over all of Jerusalem and instilling the boldness of a lion into those first Christians. Three thousand onlookers were so moved by the presence of God that they committed their lives to Christ that day, not two months after Jesus had been crucified. All fear was dissolved as the presence of the Holy Spirit hovered over those in the city. The fear of God now filled them instead of the fear of man. Because their hearts now understood that the power of God was in them and nothing was impossible. So the testimony of Jesus Christ began.

It is interesting that the testimony of Jesus Christ began with the coming of the Holy Spirit. Many people had already seen and testified of the miracles they had received or witnessed, and John the Baptist had been telling of the coming of Jesus Christ for some time already, so what was different? The difference was that now the apostles were filled with the Holy Spirit and fulfilling what Jesus said when He told them that they would do all the things that He had done and greater still. Now they were traveling from town to town, teaching what Jesus had taught them about the Kingdom of God and performing

---

[2] "Lion of Judah" Revelation 5:5 ESV "And one of the elders said to me, 'Weep no more; behold, the Lion of the tribe of Judah, the Root of David, has conquered, so that he can open the scroll and its seven seals.'"

miracles in Jesus' name. Their testimonies were not only words but contained the dunamis power of the Holy Spirit. The same power with which Jesus had healed the lame, cleansed lepers, and raised the dead, now resided in them. Jesus had given them authority before He ascended to heaven, but now they had the Spirit of God residing within them instead of just resting upon them.

Water, Spirit, Fire

Until that time, the apostles were healing, casting out demons and cleansing lepers under Jesus' authority and by drawing the kingdom of God near to them (resting upon them) but the Holy Spirit was not abiding within them. This infilling of the Holy Spirit was different from the water baptisms the crowds had been receiving from John the Baptist. Their water baptisms were for repentance and forgiveness of sins that they had committed against God, but no power came with their water baptism. The very word baptism defined the process that was happening. Baptism in Jesus' day commonly referred to the process of dying wool. The wool was fully immersed into the water and dye color that was desired. The wool would stay immersed until it had fully taken on the color of the dye through every strand, usually about three days. The people being baptized by John the Baptist were repenting for their sinful ways, but they still had not been receiving the Holy Spirit up to that point. Only Jesus Himself actually received the Holy Spirit and power at His baptism because He was already without sin.

Today water baptism is the process (sacrament)[3] of fully taking on the likeness of Jesus. Our old stained spirit gets washed clean of everything that is not pure (sinful), and it is created as brand new in Christ. We take on all of Jesus' perfect characteristics and leave all of our impure selves behind. It is our outward sign of repentance for any and all rebellion against God. We ask God to forgive all our sins; we profess our faith in Jesus Christ and His resurrection, we leave our old behaviors behind in the water and receive Jesus' Holy Spirit into our spirits.

Later in His ministry, Jesus tried to explain about the Holy Spirit to the religious elders of His day, saying, "Most assuredly, I say to you, unless one is born of water and the Spirit, he cannot enter the kingdom of God" (John 3:5 NKJV). Sadly, they did not understand what Jesus was trying to explain to them because they had never experienced the Holy Spirit indwelling in them. But when the Holy Spirit came and indwelled the apostles on Pentecost, all of that changed. The apostles became emboldened by the Spirit to speak the word of God and teach about the Messiah, Jesus Christ. The Apostle Peter began explaining to the crowds that had gathered around where the rushing, roaring wind sound was emanating from, telling them that what was happening was actually what had been prophesied by the Prophet Joel years before saying, "In the last days, God says, I will pour out My Spirit on all people. Your sons and daughters will prophesy" (Acts 2:17 NIV).

---

[3] "Sacrament" a Christian rite such as baptism that is believed to have been ordained by Christ and that is held to be a means of divine grace or to be a sign or symbol of a spiritual reality.

That's exactly what God had done. He had poured out His Spirit upon the people, and they were filled with the Holy Spirit. The apostles and those gathered in that upper room with them could no longer contain their zeal for Jesus and started prophesying over the people present, telling them of all the things God was going to do with them and through them. They extolled dozens of stories about what Jesus had done and prophesied what was coming. They laid hands on the sick, and they were healed; they cast out demons, cleansed lepers, and raised the dead, all in the name of Jesus and by the power of the Holy Spirit. They started what has now become the Christian faith.

There was another very unusual thing that happened that day as well. The apostles and others gathered in the upper room started speaking in all different types of languages. The people who had gathered at the sound of the rushing wind marveled at this phenomenon, wondering how it was possible that these Galileans could speak in multiple languages. The Holy Spirit had made it possible for them to speak in multiple languages (both then and now referred to as speaking in tongues), thus allowing for people from all the regions near and far away from Jerusalem to understand what the apostles were saying so that they might believe in Jesus Christ as the Messiah, and receive Him as their Lord and Savior. But what does this all have to do with you? You thought I forgot about you, didn't you? Nah, I knew you were still there.

What you may not yet realize is that God has been preparing you all your life, whether young or old, to be Jesus' disciple too. Everything you have learned or yearned for was to prepare you to be a follower of Christ and to spread the Good News of Jesus Christ to the world. It may just be to the little corner of your world, or it may to be the nations of the world around you. Regardless, you have a call on your life, and that call is from Jesus Himself. He wants you, and He paid the ultimate price of His life to secure yours both now and eternally. But just like the original apostles you too need the power of the Holy Spirit to accomplish all that Jesus has written in your book of life in heaven. So how does that happen?

Let me back up just a bit and be sure that you have received your initial full-immersion baptism in Jesus' name. If not, you should start there. At the risk of sounding a bit legalistic, I encourage you to have a full-immersion baptism.[4] Over the years, the rite or sacrament of baptism has taken on different forms, and in places or times when water was scarce, sprinkling became acceptable. However, if that is not your case, I heartily encourage you to have a full, bubbles over your head, immersion baptism. It is the outward sign of your faith in Jesus Christ as your Lord and Savior and the washing away the old sinful ways and being created new in Jesus. I also strongly believe that you should be baptized in the name of Jesus Christ since He is the only way into eternal life in the kingdom of God. Acts 2:38-39 NIV clearly states, "Peter replied, "Repent and be baptized, every one of you, in the name of Jesus Christ for the forgiveness of your sins, and you will receive the gift of the Holy Spirit. This promise belongs to you and your children and to all who are far off—to all whom the Lord our God will call to Himself."

---

[4] "Full-immersion baptism." Baptism by immersion is understood by some to imply submersion of the whole body beneath the surface of the water.

Then we have the infilling of the Holy Spirit part next. Acts 2 recounts the story of Pentecost and the Holy Spirit infilling of the apostles with power. If Jesus thought it was important enough to tell the apostles to wait for the Holy Spirit to infill them, then that's good enough for me. But how exactly do you make an appointment with the Holy Spirit? Is there a long waiting list? Do I need 120 friends to come to the party, and should I batten down the hatches? Nope, He's ready, willing, and able, and He keeps His own calendar. The Holy Spirit is the third person of the Triune Godhead, and He, like Jesus, is sent by the Father to help us navigate this earthly world. Just as the Bible is our earthly GPS, the Holy Spirit is our spiritual GPS, always pointing us in the direction of Jesus Christ, for He alone is the way. John 3:5 ESV says, "Jesus answered, "Most assuredly, I say to you; unless one is born of water and the Spirit, he cannot enter the kingdom of God."

As I have already mentioned, on Pentecost, not only was there the sound of a rushing wind and apostles prophesying, they were also speaking in different languages. This has long been held as the primary sign that you have been filled or born of the Spirit, the Holy Spirit, that is, but my experience was a bit reversed. I was sprinkle baptized as an infant and didn't know for another fifty years that people still spoke in tongues. I was dumbfounded to find out that anyone besides the apostles spoke in tongues, let alone still today. My Catholic upbringing never broached the subject, and I was certainly no apostle, so I never even dreamed this was possible. However, one day a co-worker mentioned that she prayed in tongues. I was fascinated! I asked her all about it and how she came to receive this gift as she was not an apostle either. She was, however, raised

Pentecostal. So I thought, *well, I must have to change over to that religious sect, and then I'll receive it too.* Made sense at the time. Pentecost = Pentecostal, right?

Thankfully that was not necessary. My co-worker explained that she simply prayed, "Come Holy Spirit, come," and she received the gift of tongues. Wow! I could hardly wait to get home and pray. And pray I did, over and over and over, but nothing was happening. Maybe I needed to be in church, or on my knees, or maybe I missed something in the prayer. It's a pretty short prayer, I'm pretty sure I got it right. Not entirely daunted, I prayed on some more. I knew the apostles had to wait on the Holy Spirit, so I kept praying and kept waiting. *Hmmm, just how long does this take?* I had no frame of reference for this after-Pentecost tongues process other than that short little prayer. With only that insight, I prayed on. I was not going to be denied.

I may have dozed off a couple of times but after several hours, I was hoarse, and my mouth parched. This Holy Spirit tongues thing was harder than I thought it was going be. Maybe I really wasn't holy enough, or maybe I needed to clarify some things with my co-worker. But like the persistent widow of scripture,[5] I pressed on just a bit longer, and guess what? I started to hear a loud wind blowing behind my house. I'm not kidding, and I'm not exaggerating. It sounded like a freight train was coming through my backyard. I turned around to look out the back window, fearful that the huge trees just behind my house may fall over and hit my house. I fully expected to see the trees

[5] Luke 18:1-8 NIV "The Parable of the Persistent Widow."

flailing about, but they were perfectly still, but the sound was still abundantly clear.

Finally, it dawned on me, "It's the Holy Spirit coming!" I didn't expect the rushing wind part; the co-worker didn't mention a thing about that. But I knew it had to be Him, and it was! A language I had never learned or even heard before came flying out of my mouth. I realized then that I had never heard tongues before, so I was totally enthralled with this phenomenon. I just sat and let this language pour out of me. I didn't have to do anything; it just kept coming forth. After a little while, the language distinctly changed to a different language. Cool! I didn't know you could get more than one other language. Guess all my persistence was really paying off. Then it changed again, and again, and again. *Hey, how do you turn this thing off?*

> *I realized then that I had never heard tongues before, so I was totally enthralled with this phenomenon*

It only now occurred to me that I didn't know how to stop this thing, and it didn't seem to be slowing down any. After two hours and at least twelve different languages, including an Ethiopian-like clucking, I finally passed out. I guess that's one way to stop it. When I came to, I firmly determined that I was going to have a stern conversation with said co-worker about giving me all the details about this tongues thing. *How's a person supposed to know what they're doing without all the details?* The next morning I quickly engaged my co-worker for all the rest of the details. No wonder the apostles were so stunned. I wondered, *Did Jesus give them all the details?*

My co-worker was quite amused with my retelling of the preceding evening's events. I wasn't sharing her amusement. She explained that she had never heard of anyone hearing the rushing wind, so that came as much of a surprise to her as me. She then gave me a very short instruction for stopping the tongues, "Shut your mouth." Feeling pretty stupid now, I much more humbly asked, "Well do I have to pray for two hours every time I want this thing to work?" She assured me that was not the case. She said that you just have to desire to pray in tongues, and it just comes out. She added, "I pray in tongues in the car every morning on my way to work." *What! You can pray tongues in the car? I was flabbergasted! Wasn't that sacrilegious or even dangerous?* I was so naive about so many things back then, but it's all true. I simply didn't know what I didn't know. I was going to have to build up a lot more confidence before I risked life and limb praying in tongues in the car.

After a couple more times of "controlled" praying in tongues, I decided I would make the big attempt of praying in tongues in the car. So that morning (better not to risk trying it at night), I made a deal with the Holy Spirit that I was going to open my mouth, and He would gently allow my prayer language in tongues to quietly come out. Not sure why I thought quietly was safer, but I wasn't taking any undue risks just yet. And I made the Holy Spirit promise He wouldn't veer me off the road and crash when it came forth. I'm pretty sure I was driving about 10 miles an hour when I took the big risk and opened my mouth. And (drum roll)…taa-daa, it worked! Tongues commenced, and I stayed on the road as people jogged by me.

It's all very funny to me now as I think back to those first moments of encountering the Holy Spirit. I have no doubt Jesus, the Holy Spirit, and a whole bunch of angels got a chuckle out of my innocent beginnings. I tell you all of that because there really is no way of "controlling" the Holy Spirit. There is no one way that He shows up in your life. There is no perfect recipe for receiving the infilling of the Holy Spirit. Since my innocent beginning, I have prayed with many people who don't even get past "Come Holy" and tongues begins coming forth from them. I have already baptized people who come up out of the water praying in tongues, and nobody prayed for it. The Holy Spirit is our Helper, and He shows up when we need Him and in His perfect timing. I must admit, though, that I'm still wondering about the Ethiopian-like clucking language. *Hmmm?*

In case you forgot what I was initially explaining, I received my gift of tongues before I was full-immersion baptized. Several years later, after a minister friend of mine had encouraged me to do a full-immersion baptism, I felt an overwhelming need to be baptized the way they did it in Jesus' day. I was fortuitously on my boat at a nearby lake. All day long, I had such a burning in my heart that I just had to be baptized that day, so I called my dear minister friend and suggested to her a rather unconventional idea. I asked her if I put my cell phone on speaker and placed it on the deck of the boat, would she just say the baptismal words over me, and I would go in the lake and fully immerse myself declaring my repentance and belief in Jesus my Lord and Savior. Much to my surprise, she said, "I'll be right there." I reminded her that she was at work two hours away from where I was. She said, "Never mind that; I'll be there as soon as I can."

And true to her word, two hours later, she showed up on the docks. I picked her up along with another dear friend who came to celebrate this special event with me. We moored up in the quiet, beautiful cove where I had spent countless weekends just communing with nature and God. It was one of my favorite places of peace and tranquility to pray and talk with God. The one friend stayed on the boat and took pictures while my minister friend and I went in the water. I need to paint a full picture here, though. I was wearing a bathing suit, but my friend had come right from work in a dress, heels, and stockings. No matter, stockings, dress, and all, in she went with me and full-immersion baptized me in the name of Jesus Christ. While there was no church, no pomp and circumstance, no procession or robes, it was every bit as holy and the declaration every bit as sincere and binding.

There's a funny thing about the Holy Spirit—He's contagious. Whenever He shows up, people are touched around you. My friend who was taking pictures to commemorate the day was likewise touched. With tears in her eyes, she put down the camera and stepped into the water, also fully dressed. "Baptize me," she emotionally requested, and my minister friend turned to me and said, "Baptize her." Still dripping wet from my own baptism, I slowly walked my friend through repentance and her declaration of belief in Jesus Christ and immersed her in the quiet, still waters of the lake. It was impossible to tell the difference between our tears and the droplets of lake water still running down our faces. But it was undeniable that the Holy Spirit had entered our hearts and moved us deeply. I will never forget that day, and that cove will be forever marked with the outward profession of our faith in Jesus Christ.

Later I mused at the thought of the fish in the lake that day being made doubly holy, and it reminded me of the Bible story of when Simon Peter had first met Jesus and cast his nets into the water making a staggering catch of fish.[6] I secretly asked Jesus in my heart if maybe someday I could make such a symbolic catch of souls along those very same banks of the lake. Baptizing hundreds, if not thousands, of people just as I had been baptized under an open heaven filled with the Holy Spirit descending on all of them. I wait in anxious anticipation of the day, knowing that all of God's answers are yes and amen.[7]

As I mentioned at the beginning of this section, once the Holy Spirit infilled the apostles, as they spread the Good News of Jesus Christ, they now were laying hands on the sick and healing them, casting out demons, cleansing lepers, and raising the dead all in the name of Jesus through the power of the Holy Spirit abiding in them. That same Holy Spirit power abides in every Christian believer today, and while I know there is much debate among religious orders regarding the Holy Spirit, baptism, speaking in tongues, and the power gifts of the Holy Spirit, the point to be learned here is that regardless of how all the timing works out, we need to wait on the Holy Spirit and

---

[6] John 21:1-14 BSB "Jesus Appears by the Sea of Tiberias."

[7] 2 Corinthians 1:20 NKJV "For all the promises of God in Him are Yes, and in Him Amen, to the glory of God through us."

the infilling power He brings us because Jesus then told His disciples and all of us, "Go into all the world and preach the Good News to everyone." (Mark 16:15 NLT) And that's exactly what I'm encouraging you to do.

There is one additional baptism I will mention here just so you know it exists, and that is the baptism of fire. In Luke 3:16 NKJV, John the Baptist explained to the people saying, "I indeed baptize you with water; but One mightier than I is coming, whose sandal strap I am not worthy to loose. He will baptize you with the Holy Spirit and fire." So we have Holy Spirit prophesy, tongues, power, and now fire. Thankfully this baptism does not immerse you in flames, well, at least not in the natural. Many believers may never experience this baptism, but for some, it generally comes with spiritual maturity and often is tied to the level of ministry that the Lord has planned for you. It is a spiritual purification process that prepares you for a more advanced level of ministry. While I have gone through this baptism as well, it's probably a story for another book. I'll just say that it is a very intense encounter with the Holy Spirit and usually brings with it an upgrade in gifts and anointing to equip you for the work the Lord is preparing you to do.

Gifts, Talents, and Anointings

In addition to the power gifts of the Holy Spirit, we can receive many other gifts, talents, and anointings from the Holy Spirit to accomplish the tasks that God has set in our destinies. Some of the other gifts of the Holy Spirit[8] mentioned throughout

---

[8] 1 Corinthians 12:1-11 ESV "Spiritual Gifts."

the Bible are words of wisdom, words of knowledge, faith, distinguishing between spirits, and interpretation of tongues. Some gifts seem to manifest as talents that can be used to build up the church, such as teaching, exhortation, giving, leadership, service, and mercy. Still others are anointed to be apostles, prophets, evangelists, pastors, or teachers. All are necessary and essential to the successful working of the Church.

God has equipped all of us with different gifts, talents, and anointing, and that includes you. No one has been left out. You may not yet recognize the gifts or talents, but I assure you they are there, or they are on their way. Everything God placed in us, whether at birth, baptism or later are for His glory and the building up the Church for winning souls for Christ. When Jesus' love overflows in us, we want every single person to share in the everlasting joy of eternal life with Christ. I learned this lesson in a rather sobering way. Let me tell you that story.

One morning as I was preparing to leave for work, the Lord asked me a question. "Sue, do you love me?" As indignantly as Simon had answered Jesus when he was asked the same question.[9] I answered, "Yes, of course, I love you, Jesus." Then He asked me if I thought I could bring five souls to Him for salvation. "Yes, Lord, I'm sure I can bring five souls to salvation." Again, as I was getting into the car, Jesus asked me if maybe I thought I could bring Him fifty souls. Again, I repeated, "Yes, Lord, I'm pretty sure I can bring fifty souls to salvation." Heading down the street towards the college where I worked, Jesus pressed me yet again. "How about 500?" I was getting irritated now. So

[9] John 21:15-17 "Jesus Reinstates Peter."

through somewhat gritted teeth, I answered, "Yes, Jesus, even 500 seems possible." He was quiet for a little while, and then He spoke again, "How about 5,000?" *Really,* I thought, but to tell you the truth, I had to think about that for a minute. I'd only led a couple of people to the Lord at that time, so 5,000 was a pretty good stretch for me. I was quiet for a minute and then bolstered up my courage and proudly announced, "Yes, even 5,000!" *Well, that should shut Him up now.* Nope!

As I neared the university, I had to drive by their massive football stadium, which seated over 100,000 people, and as Jesus spoke my name, I knew the next number in His series was going to be 50,000, so in a flash to beat Him to the punch I blurted out, "Aw hell, Lord, let's just fill up the stadium and I'll lead them to You a hundred thousand at a time!" Victory! I was feeling so proud of myself for my courageous, albeit grandiose commitment. (And yes, I did say hell to Jesus. He wasn't too phased by it.) The Lord responded, "Okay, I like that number." I was just as pleased as punch with myself. Then the Lord said, "But I have just one more question for you, Sue." "Okay, what's that?" I said with a little bit of trepidation. The Lord continued, "If I only ever needed you to bring just one person to me for salvation, could you be satisfied with that? Because Sue, every *one* matters to me."

Kapow! I felt like I was hit with a sledgehammer. My pride had gotten the better of me but Jesus' heart brought me to the reality that ***every single soul*** is tremendously important and not to be trivialized. And perhaps the plan Jesus wrote for us only involves bringing one person to Christ in our whole lives.

But that one person is as important to Jesus as the millions some evangelists bring to salvation on the plains of Africa. This is a lesson I will never forget! It is the lesson I live my life by. Every *one* matters!

My dear fellow citizens of earth, you matter, the guy or girl next to you matters, the old lady down the street matters, and the homeless guy under the bridge on the rough side of town matters. And maybe, just maybe, they are your *one*. You may not have clever words or fancy linen robes, but God has called you to gather in His harvest of souls. No matter how many or how few gifts, talents, or anointings you may have, **you are equipped** for this job! You are fully ready and able because the One who lives inside of you is fully ready and able. The Holy Spirit is all you need.

So I encourage you to think about how your talents might help someone find their way to Jesus or spread the Gospel. You might be an artist or author; a singer or violinist; a carpenter or designer. You might love to read or public speaking; tinkering or creating; typing or calculating. They are all highly usable gifts or talents you can use for God's kingdom. No matter how huge or small your talents or endeavors are, God can use them, and He wants you to be a part of what He is doing on the earth, here and now. You may still be wondering where your harvest field is, to which I say: the neighborhood streets, the hospitals, the schools, businesses, stadiums, or the massive expanses of Africa, India, China, and the rest of the world are waiting for you. You don't have to change the world; you just need to change a life. Just one life!

Transformed Mind

You have probably heard this old Chinese proverb, "A journey of a thousand miles begins with a single step."[10] Meaning that no matter how far you have to go, you've got to start by taking a single step. No matter how far you think you are from God, you really are only one step away; the first one. Actually, you are only one thought away from Him because what you are thinking determines what step you are going to take next. Good or bad, wise or foolish, fast or slow, happy or sad, brilliant or not-too-shiny, our thoughts control our actions. As a matter of fact, they control our emotions, feelings, and responses. So your journey of a thousand miles begins with a single thought: I can or I can't.

Climbing Mount Everest starts with a single step. Swimming the English Channel begins with a single step into the water. Breaking the four-minute mile began with a single step. And who could ever forget one of the most iconic of all single steps: "One small step for man, one giant leap for mankind."[11] Right now, you may think there's just no way that you can turn your life around; that's just too big a leap for you. But I'd

---

[10] "The Journey of a Thousand Miles" The quotation is from Chapter 64 of the Dao De Jing ascribed to Laozi, although it is also erroneously ascribed to his contemporary, Confucius. This saying teaches that even the longest and most difficult ventures have a starting point; something which begins with one first step. Retrieved from: https://en.wikipedia.org/wiki/A_journey_of_a_thousand_miles_begins_with_a_single_step. Accessed 13 August 2021.

[11] Neil Alden Armstrong (August 5, 1930 – August 25, 2012) was an American astronaut and aeronautical engineer, and the first person to walk on the Moon. Retrieved from: https://en.wikipedia.org/wiki/Neil_Armstrong#First_Moon_walk. Accessed 13 August 2021.

like to challenge that thought response and remind you that nothing is impossible with God. That you can do all things through Christ who strengthens you. (Philippians 4:13 NKJV) The very first step is transforming your thoughts. I can't can be changed to I can with a single thought. Every change that ever happened in the world started with someone thinking, "I can." I can climb, swim, run, jump, or whatever faster, higher, or longer than that. Your only limitation is what you're thinking.

Romans 12:2 NLT says, "Don't copy the behavior and customs of this world, but let God transform you into a new person by changing the way you think. Then you will learn to know God's will for you, which is good and pleasing and perfect." You know that good 'ole Bible has an answer for everything. So why do we always seem to think of all the reasons we can't do something? It clearly does not align with God's word, so we know it's not from Him. It's worldly thinking. We are usually conformed into the behavior of the world around us. If you don't live in a third-world country, you are likely bombarded constantly with advertising and marketing campaigns telling you what is good, pleasing, and perfect and that unfortunately seldom lines up with what God thinks. So how do we get rid of all that stink'n think'n?

Second Corinthians 10:5 BSB gives us the precise answer. "We tear down arguments and every presumption set up against the knowledge of God; and we take captive every thought to make it obedient to Christ." Essentially we need to dismantle what the world tells us is good and make every single thought align with what Jesus says about us instead. If God thinks it's a good idea, then it's a good idea—go with it. If God says, "Hey, don't do that!"

Then, don't do that! This isn't rocket science here. Remember God is love, peace, mercy, forgiveness, and all that is good. If you're thinking about loving someone, forgiving someone, or making peace with someone, you're on the right track.

Yes, I realize that more than likely, you have been hurt somewhere along the line in your life and perhaps even very badly mistreated, but you have the free will choice about how you are going to think about all of that. While you may not be able to forget those hurts, you can choose to forgive them. While you may have been abandoned by your natural parents, God never abandoned you. You get to choose which one of those things you want to dwell on and believe. While you may have been an outcast in your neighborhood, school clique, or even country, God has claimed you as His own and made you an heir to all that He has. The choice of what you are going to believe is yours, not the world's.

In Dr. Caroline Leaf's book *Switch On Your Brain, The Key to Peak Happiness, Thinking and Health,*[12] she explains how our minds create and process thoughts and the subsequent pathways that become established in our brains. The more frequently we entertain the same thought, the more ingrained the pathway becomes established in our brains. So it stands to reason if you have been repeatedly told you are weak, unlovable, worthless, incapable, too tall, too short, too thin, too round, too dumb, too flighty, too whatever, your mind has created a well-worn path for storing that thought, memory, feeling or emotional

---

[12] Caroline Leaf, *Switch On Your Brain, The Key to Peak Happiness, Thinking and Health* (Grand Rapids, MI: Baker Books a division of Baker Publishing Group, 2013).

tie. Oh, that the world would tell us more of what God says about us instead because that is exactly what needs to happen to change your stink'n think'n.

As I have made it abundantly clear throughout this book, the Holy Bible is God's written truth about you and everything in your life, world, and universe. It is the truth about everything that has ever happened, is happening, or will happen. It's the perfect place to go to start transforming your mind and taking every thought captive to what Christ has done for you, thinks of you, and wants for you. Declaring what God has said about you in the Bible will create new, correct pathways in your mind. Due to the past years of repetition, the change won't be overnight because the old pathways are so ingrained in your mind, but when you can accept that you are replacing the lies with the truth, you will succeed. You will begin to see yourself through God's eyes as the incredible person He created you to be. There's an added bonus to this replacement of lies. You will start to see the rest of the world through the eyes of God as well.

> *The Holy Bible is God's written truth about you and everything in your life, world, and universe*

What we think or believe is our reality. Make what God says about you your reality because it is true. From where you are standing, it may not seem very likely, but you won't be the first one to think that way. Judges tells the story of Gideon and how the Israelites had been greatly oppressed by the Midianites. One day the angel of the Lord appears to Gideon and says, "The Lord is with you, O mighty man of valor." While it sounds like a pretty cool thing to have said to you, it seemed a bit contradictory to the situation because at the time, Gideon was hiding in a wine press from the marauding Midianites; not exactly the picture of a mighty man of valor. Gideon argues with the angel (a word to the wise: It's never a good idea to argue with an angel of the Lord), saying, "How can that be true because my clan is the weakest in Manasseh, and I am the youngest in my father's house?"

Gideon only believed his current circumstances instead of what God was saying about him and even after God proved His promise to Gideon in repeated miracles, Gideon still snuck around in the dark doing what God had instructed him to do. We often feel and think the same way. How can things be different from what they are now? The answer is simple: Because God is greater than our circumstances. When you trust in what God has said, you can't be stopped. That's where all your power comes from—God. Whether God the Father, Jesus the Son, or the Holy Spirit, when God is for you no one can be against you. Which further extrapolated means no one can stop you. So believe what God has said about you and watch the change in you happen. By the way, Gideon went on to take out the Midianites and be the mighty man of valor God called him to be. So who has God called you to be?

Walking in Your Authority

Depending on what God has called you to be will impact the equipping you will need, but the authority will always be the same. The apostles preached, healed, cleansed, and raised the dead all in Jesus' name and His authority. In Matthew 28:18 NLT, Jesus came and told His disciples, "I have been given all authority in heaven and on earth." Then in Luke 10:19 ESV, Jesus turns around and gives us His authority when He says, "Behold, I give you the authority to trample on serpents and scorpions, and over all the power of the enemy, and nothing shall by any means hurt you." And once you know that Bible verse, it makes the devil tremble in fear. If you have ever thought you were powerless against what the world was throwing at you, I want to dispel that lie right here and now. You are not powerless by any means. Every believer who testifies to Christ as their Lord and Savior is power "full" and Satan knows it, and now so do you.

Friends, the God of the whole universe has given you authority over **ALL** the power of the enemy (Satan). When you accepted Christ, you received this authority. All of it! Honestly, that's staggering to even contemplate. (Go ahead, contemplate that for a minute. I'll wait.) Okay, that was fun, wasn't it? Just like the police officer who puts up one hand and brings you to a stop, you can put up one hand and bring all of Satan's demonic little friends to a stop by the authority invested in you by Jesus Christ. When you name-drop Jesus' name, you bring Satan to his knees. As a matter of fact, all of creation must bow its knee to the name of Jesus.[13] Pretty cool, huh?

Just as there is authority in the natural physical world that we live in, so too there is authority in the spiritual world that we are

---

[13] "Therefore God exalted Him to the highest place and gave Him the name above all names, that at the name of Jesus every knee should bow, in heaven and on earth and under the earth, and every tongue confess that Jesus Christ is Lord, to the glory of God the Father." Philippians 2:9-11 BSB

a part of as well. Our physical world has challenges of all kinds. Some we can easily overcome in the physical, but some need a higher authority. That's when we need Jesus' authority. Like people who get on our nerves in the natural, there are spirits that try to drive us bonkers in the spiritual realm. The truly fantastic part of receiving Jesus' authority is that it is equally enforceable in both the natural and the spiritual worlds. But we need to learn how to exercise that authority in the spiritual realm as well as the natural world.

We need to learn how things function in the heavenlies to know how to operate effectively there. Here's something cool to know. When something is fixed in heaven, it gets fixed here on earth. It's a twofer![14] Since demons are spiritual beings, they operate out of the spiritual realm to affect us here in the natural realm. The Bible tells us, "For though we live in the flesh [world], we do not wage war according to the flesh [world]. The weapons of our warfare are not the weapons of the world. Instead, they have divine power to demolish strongholds" (2 Corinthians 10:3-4 BSB). All of which means we need to understand what weapons we're supposed to be using to harness divine power. And lucky for us, it's all written in one book. Yup, you guessed right again, the Holy Bible. We need to use the Word of God to destroy the works of the devil here on earth.

I tell you all of this, so you comprehend both the power and authority you have been gifted but also to instill in you

---

[14] Twofer: 1.) two articles available for the price of one or about the price of one. 2). something that satisfies two criteria or needs simultaneously. Retrieved from https://www.merriam-webster.com/dictionary/twofer. Accessed on 5 May 2021.

that you're not alone in your battles and you are not defeated. God has not only given you the power and authority, but He has also given you the instruction manual for how to use them effectively in every single aspect of your life, no matter what you may currently be believing. Believing is the key to unlocking all of God's promises. What you believe in your mind, soul, and spirit are what authority and power you walk in. God has made provisions for every challenge you might face in your life—bar none.

In addition to helping you overcome the problems you may face, God also wants you to help change the world around you too. Remember the part "It's not about you"? All power and authority are to be used for the good of God's kingdom. We can speak God's Word and see our life circumstances change, and we can speak God's Word over others and see their life circumstances change too. Another twofer! God's abundance in action. It may surprise you to know that you have all authority over the devil, but the Bible makes it very clear in Mark 16:15-17 NIV, "And He said to them, "Go into all the world and preach the gospel to every creature. Whoever believes and is baptized will be saved, but whoever does not believe will be condemned. And these signs will accompany those who believe: In My name they will drive out demons; they will speak in new tongues."

Astoundingly, the first thing Jesus tells His disciples is that whoever believes and is baptized will drive out demons! And before you go getting side-tracked on the word demons, please know that they don't show up as little red devils with pitchforks. Rather they show up in the stink'n think'n thoughts you have.

The ones that tell you you're not good enough, shame you, torment you, frighten you, or an endless list of things that do not align with what God says about you. That's where they always begin, in what you think and believe. They want to twist the truth and deceive you into believing lies about who you are and what authority you walk in, knowing full well that if you know and believe the truth about your authority, they're sunk. They don't have a leg to stand on (or a pitchfork either)!

I want to point out something else important here. Jesus said "whoever" believes has this authority. That means you and I, as believers, can walk in this authority. The reason is because, as believers, we are seated in heavenly places with Jesus. "And God raised us up with Christ and seated us with Him in the heavenly realms in Christ Jesus" (Ephesians 2:6 NIV). We literally share Jesus' seat of authority in heaven. As I mentioned earlier, when things are fixed in heaven, they also get fixed on earth. Since we as believer's hold a place in both the physical and the spiritual worlds, we are the conduits to make that happen. Remembering that Jesus already told us that we would do all the things He did and greater still.[15] Folks, that is the authority you should be walking in.

Before we go too far astray here, this whole dialogue has been to encourage you that you can overcome all the thoughts that hold you back from walking in freedom and authority over your circumstances. There is a great deal more to learn about our Christian authority but for now, know that you, as

---

[15] "Very truly I tell you, whoever believes in Me will do the works I have been doing, and they will do even greater things than these, because I am going to the Father." John 14:12 NIV

a believer, are already empowered to defeat anything that is trying to pull you away from what God has said about you and that Jesus has already won for you.

Miracles, Signs, and Wonders

In the last section, I discussed the authority that Jesus gave His disciples and us to work miracles of healing, casting out demons, cleansing lepers, and raising the dead. We don't hear a lot about that on the nightly news or even in most of the western culture churches today. There aren't that many lepers walking around anymore, and raising the dead just plain sounds creepy unless, of course, it's someone you dearly love. Depending on your circumstances, a miracle healing may be the only way you stay alive, and well, there's more demons oppressing people than you could possibly imagine. (I'm just say'n!) But I want to relay a few personal stories about the miracles, signs, and wonders that I have seen over the years, so you know that they still are in effect today and are still as powerful as they were in Jesus' day.

I've already told you about the wonder of the tree and flowers returning overnight, and the blood clots miraculously disappearing overnight, and there are so many more I could tell you about, but I just want to pick a few to emphasize the most significant point of this book. So come walk with me down memory lane for a few minutes.

One of the first creative healing miracles I ever witnessed was in June of 2016. You tend to remember the dates of creative healing miracles because they impact your life so much and the life of the person being healed. There was a woman who had severely crippled hands from arthritis. She had asked me to pray that her hands might be straightened so that she could actually function normally again. This happened at a local fast-food restaurant. Jesus never was a respecter of eating establishments. So I took the lady's hands and covered them in mine and began to pray a simple prayer for healing in Jesus' name. That was until I realized I was asking God to straighten all the bones in this lady's hands. Up until this time, I had only been praying for headaches, backaches, and sore knees and joints. This was going to be life-changing for this lady, and honestly, I was scared to death of Jesus not coming through for her.

As my mind raced around a million miles an hour inside my head, I prayed and prayed and prayed everything I could think of to pray. This was no longer a simple prayer, and I was getting a bit panic-stricken. Then softly, I heard Jesus say to me, "You know sooner or later you're going to have to let go of that lady's hands. Are you going to trust Me or not?" Jesus had me dead to rights. Either I was going to trust Him for the miracle or not. Which was it going to be? So as any youngster is want to do, I hedged my bet with Jesus. I said, "Jesus can You show me what her hands look like in heaven?" And graciously, He did. They were perfectly straight and picture-perfectly beautiful. Then I made a deal with Jesus. I bargained with Him, saying, "Okay, Jesus, I'm going to trust You and let go of this lady's hands, and that's exactly what I want them to look like, okay?" Hah! I had Jesus on the ropes now.

Jesus didn't pause for a second and quietly said, "Okay." So slowly, ever so slowly, I slid my hands back off of the lady's hands, and (really long drum roll here) they were perfectly healed just like the hands Jesus had shown me! Praise God! Hallelujah! I jumped up out of my seat like I was shot out of a cannon, nearly knocking the whole table over. I jumped up and down, yelling and screaming like I was on fire. "They're healed, they're healed!" I was beyond ecstatic. You would have thought I was the one that got healed. Needless to say, the lady was really excited too. I told everybody in the restaurant, all of whom probably thought I was totally loony. It didn't matter; Jesus healed her hands. Did I mention that my faith also shot up like it was shot out of that cannon with me? Miracles have a way of doing that to you, you know.

Then there was the time that my very old horse Archie got sick. He had gotten a puncture wound on his right shoulder, and it wasn't healing. He kept getting sicker and sicker until finally, the veterinarian said she couldn't do anything else and that he would have to be euthanized. I had rescued this horse more than ten years before and hated to see him suffer any longer. I asked the veterinarian to give me one more day so that I could make the necessary arrangements for his body. She agreed. I cried my heart out for this sweet old horse and hated to have to be the one to make such a decision.

That night around midnight, Jesus woke me up and asked me why I hadn't laid hands on the horse and prayed for his healing. In all my dismay, it had never even occurred to me to pray healing over my horse. Hard to believe, but it was true. Jesus said, "Go lay hands on your horse and pray for him to be well." "Now?" I asked incredulously. "Yes, now," Jesus replied.

So at midnight, I got out of bed, pulled some jeans up over my pajamas, slipped on some muck boots, and went to the barn. Poor Archie could not even lift his head anymore. He was leaned up against the stall wall struggling with every breath. He hadn't eaten or drunk anything for several days. I knew he didn't have long to live, and it ripped at my heart to see him this way.

With tears streaming down my face, I gently placed my hands on his neck and smoothed over his coat which was so dull and lifeless now. I whispered my love to him, but he couldn't even turn his head to listen. I prayed softly, imploring Jesus to heal my friend or put him out of his misery. One way or another, I couldn't see him suffer this way anymore. I kissed him on the neck and told him goodbye. Very early the following morning, I got a phone call from the folks who owned the barn where my horse was boarded just across the street. I knew that a call that early meant my friend had died in the night and that they had found him dead in his stall when they went out to feed.

With tears already running down my face, I answered the phone. "You're never going to believe what's happened!" the excited voice on the other end declared. Not at all what I was expecting but before I could even ask, "What?" The girl from the boarding stables exclaimed, "Archie's been healed! He's out running around the pasture like he's a two-year-old! We went into the barn this morning, and he was nickering and all bright-eyed and bushy-tailed and raring to go. We took him out to the pasture to let him have some grass, and he's frolicking all around the pasture. What did you do to him last night?"

I dropped to my knees and cried because I knew who had done the something to him in the night. Jesus touched him and made him whole again. I ran across the street, not bothering to pull anything on over my pjs to see my miracle horse. And there he was, running up and down in his pasture, tossing his head and flashing his tail proudly like a young colt. His coat was absolutely gleaming, and his eyes sparkled like I hadn't seen them do in years. There was no denying that miracle or resurrection because my friend was surely on his deathbed that night, and now he had new life in him that left us all in wide-eyed wonder. Praise the God who heals and gives life!

> There was no denying that miracle ... Praise God who heals and gives life!

Then fast forward a couple of years, I was on a mission trip in Brazil, and there was a man who came into the facility where we were holding the prayer sessions, and he had a grapefruit-sized goiter on the right side of his neck. I asked him the routine questions about it—when it had started, and if he was in much pain with it. The translator gave the series of questions to the man in Portuguese, and he responded in turn. No pain but a lot of discomfort simply from the size of this goiter. It filled the entire side of his neck from his jaw to his shoulder, making it nearly impossible for this man to move his head or neck. Through the translator, I asked if I could lightly place my hands on the man's neck to pray for him. He nodded ever-so-slightly, yes. The very moment my hands touched the man's neck, the goiter decreased in size so dramatically that it made me scream and jump back. It was utterly startling that the goiter literally melted under my hand. I hadn't expected such a dramatic result. I hadn't even prayed yet.

We all laughed at my very unceremonious display of shock as we all just stood there and literally watched the goiter disappear from the man's neck. He kept describing what he was feeling as the fluid flowed out of the goiter. I don't know which of us was more surprised, me or the man. The man came in fully expecting Jesus to heal him, and he was not disappointed. We hadn't even prayed, and yet he received his healing. While my faith had been taking huge leaps and bounds, God was still surprising me every day with His faithfulness to heal in His mighty name and authority. Was there nothing impossible for God? No! I was learning every day that nothing was impossible for God!

I have seen blind eyes see again, deaf ears opened, the lame jump up and dance, voices restored, cancer disappear from hands, breasts, and brains, and so many, many more things, but Jesus decided one day to show me something I had never seen before. It's no secret to anyone who knows me (and now you are included in that list) that I have a heart for the Brazilian people. They are warm, loving, and passionate about their God. They openly love Jesus and worship with such passion, it humbles me. I'm pretty sure God really loves them, too, because I have seen more miracles in Brazil than anywhere else. It's a miracle bonanza down there. I have no doubt it is because of their faith in God's desire and ability to perform them.

But there is one time that stands out to me that supersedes all of that. It's right up there as the top two most life-changing events of my life so far. The other one I've already told you was the first time God ever spoke audibly to me, and Jesus blew my religion right out the door. When God takes time out of His busy day to talk out loud to you, your life is definitely changed. Just ask Adam, Moses, or Abraham. Just wanted you to know that the bar has been set pretty high.

Again I was in Brazil, on a different mission trip. This happened in 2018. There had been a worship service, and the speaker had shared a message with the people assembled. The service was in a large church that held around 2,000 people. The church was fairly narrow but long and packed to the gills. At the end of the service, the mission team was invited to the front of the church to pray for those coming forward for the altar call. That was the plan right up until the Holy Spirit showed up and covered everyone present. Pandemonium ensued! What was a quiet procession of people coming forward turned into a chaos of people manifesting wildly under the presence of the Almighty.

Everyone started shaking and crying uncontrollably. I need to emphasize the uncontrollableness of their situation. The power of the Holy Spirit had filled them so powerfully they simply could not be still in any way, shape, or form. Their hearts were touched by a love so great that their hearts, minds, and bodies were completely overwhelmed. They cried out in a desperation, even they could not understand, but their spirits alone understood. I don't know about you, but I'd never seen such a mass infilling of the Holy Spirit before, and it was turning into total bedlam. Thankfully the speaker recognized what was happening and instructed the team to just start touching people because the Holy Spirit was already there and taking over.

Much like when people storm the field after a big game win, people started storming the mission team lined at the altar. They were so on fire with the Holy Spirit they crushed forward en-mass, flooding the aisles and pushing forward. As urgently instructed, I just started touching all the people who were shaking so uncontrollably. The power of the Holy Spirit overcame them instantaneously, and they were falling under the presence of the Spirit, except they weren't falling because they were so packed up against each other they couldn't fall to the ground. Insanity was setting in, and the fervor was increasing. I was being jostled all about by the people just wanting a touch. I thought this must have been what Jesus felt like when all the people crowded around Him wanting a healing of some sort.

Thankfully, a few of the other team members helped me continue to work my way down the aisle touching as many people as I could reach. For the people still in the rows that could not make it out into the aisles, I just reached out my hand towards them, and the Holy Spirit just laid them over one to the next like dominoes right in their seats. The indescribable power of God was beyond anything I had ever seen or experienced, and I was only halfway down the aisle. My eyes began to fill with tears, and my heart was pounding in my chest, and I said, "Lord, don't let me go out in the Spirit too. I'm only halfway." I blinked and blinked, trying to clear the tears from my eyes and keep moving forward through the sea of bodies; some upright and some not so upright.

Then time seemed to come to a standstill. I was caught in a spiritual realm that was half in the natural and half in the spiritual. I had the strangest sensations coming over me. I queried God, asking Him what He was doing and what was happening to me? And then the most unbelievable moments of my life began to happen. I began seeing through Jesus' eyes. My mind scrambled to make sense of what I was seeing and how I was seeing. Then I felt Jesus breathing through my lungs and mouth, and I felt the very hair on Jesus' arms as though they were my arms. *What in the world was happening to me?* I passionately begged Jesus to tell me what He was doing because it was starting to scare me. Jesus calmly, in the tumultuous storm of things happening around me said, "Sue, this morning you prayed that you wanted to see them through my eyes, well, now you are." There are times when things happen to you that you have no earthly explanation for, and this was one of those times. *How was this possible?* My brain was so far on overload with what was happening that I simply could not fathom it.

But Jesus wasn't done yet. As my brain was nearing meltdown, Jesus released His emotions into me as well. A tsunami flood of love, compassion, and zeal overcame me as I stood, trying to gauge the insanity that my mind was facing. "Lord, how is this possible?" I pleaded in utter desperation. The answer was not forthcoming, but it didn't really matter because the very presence of Jesus was infilling me beyond anything I could think or imagine. I was looking through Jesus' eyes at the masses of people clambering for a touch from Him. I have searched thesauruses from cover to cover to find words to describe the enormity of Jesus' emotions. I can say unequivocally; there are none!

There are no adjectives in any known language on earth that can adequately describe how much Jesus loves us, feels for us, and desires us to be joined to Him. His zeal is wildly beyond anything of measure in this world. Astronomical barely comes close to Jesus' level of compassion. The creator of the world was alive and breathing inside my body. The maker of humankind was displaying His love and passion for us, and I was paralyzed by the mere thought of it. I was gifted a rare glimpse into the heart of Jesus for all of us. The heart that willingly laid down His life to secure ours for all eternity. And I can tell you that all eternity will not be long enough to get enough of Jesus' love. Nothing in this world or the next can compare. His love is the very essence of what we were made for. That, my dear brothers and sisters in Christ, is the reason for and the most important message of this book. **His love!** Jesus' love conquers all, exceeds all, and is all that matters! There is nothing greater! Nothing!

There are no adjectives in any known
language on earth that can adequately
describe how much Jesus loves us, feels for
us, and desires us to be joined to Him.

Conclusion

A Choice to Make

Nothing is Impossible With God

When you come face to face with an impossibility, it stops you in your tracks. You then have a choice to make. You can either stay frozen, turn around and go back from where you came, or change what you think is possible. I recommend the last option because it will open your mind, your eyes, your future, and just maybe your heart to what is possible. If you think your life could never be different, better, sweeter, happier, or redeemed, I'm here to tell you that's simply not true because nothing is impossible with God. I'm living proof of that bold statement.

I bookended this book with two of the most amazing encounters of my life to give you hope at the beginning and at the end. Whether you are at the beginning of your life, trial or tragedy, or if you are nearing the end, God's not done with you yet. He's got a couple more miracles up His sleeve. Literally,

I could write a dozen more books just about the miracles, signs, and wonders I have seen in the last ten years, but more importantly, what do you have to write? Because your testimony is how you give glory to God. The Bible exhorts us to "Let the redeemed of the LORD proclaim that He has redeemed them from the power of the foe" (Psalms 107:2 HCSB).

There's a scene in the movie *Eat Pray Love*[1] starring Julia Roberts where she says to Javier Bardem, her love interest, "*Attraversiamo,*" which is Italian for "Let's cross over." Julia had to overcome her fear to surrender to love again. She had failed repeatedly at love and life, so she just couldn't seem to take that first step to believe that love could ever work out or to trust the love that was standing right in front of her. I was that same way, and you may be too. God had to first get me to believe that He was real and that He really did love me, and you may need to be convinced as well. Of course, it is best not to defy God if at all possible. A healthy dose of the fear of the Lord is actually a good thing because Proverbs 9:10 NIV tells us that "the fear of the Lord is the beginning of wisdom." Darn if those nuns weren't right about that after all. But oh, that they would have given us the Amplified version of that verse to have a better understanding. "The [reverent] fear of the LORD [that is, worshiping Him and *regarding Him as truly awesome*] is the beginning and the preeminent part of wisdom

---

[1] *"Eat Pray Love"* is a 2010 American biographical romantic drama film starring Julia Roberts as Elizabeth Gilbert, based on Gilbert's 2006 memoir of the same name. Ryan Murphy co-wrote and directed the film, which was released in the United States on August 13, 2010. (Columbia Pictures and Plan B Entertainment, 2010). Retrieved from https://en.wikipedia.org/wiki/Eat_Pray_Love. Accessed 9 May 2021.

[its starting point and its essence], and the knowledge of the Holy One is understanding and spiritual insight" (emphasis added). Because if we want to have a different life, we have to first believe that it might just be possible. Everything we do begins with a single thought. Let yours be a positive one. Offer God your first surrendered yes, and watch what happens. You just might turn out amazing!

You may also need to change the lenses you've been looking through regardless of your religious background up to this point and give Jesus the wheel to steer your life for a while. You may have crashed and burned a couple of times already in your life, but that doesn't mean that Jesus can't throw you a lifeline, recalculate your path, and show you life from a different perspective and vantage point. He truly is the only One who knows your destination because He is the only One who wrote it all out for you. Sometimes our lives take wrong turns, but there's never a bad time to make a good decision and change the direction of your life. You may need to break free from some of the people, places, or things that have been holding you back so that you can run the race that has been set before you[2] and find the fulfillment and joy that God has waiting for you.

If your heart and spirit have been banged up, bruised, or even broken, you're going to need some tender loving care (TLC) to mend them, and Jesus has more of that than even He knows what to do with. So don't be afraid to let Him cover you with His golden, mending TLC and create something incredibly

---

[2] "Therefore we also, since we are surrounded by so great a cloud of witnesses, let us lay aside every weight, and the sin which so easily ensnares us, and let us run with endurance the race that is set before us." Hebrews 12:1 NKJV

beautiful in the process. Your wounds may have created some scars, but they aren't what makes you broken. They show you have come through the battle and overcome it. They are badges of honor, and you've earned them. The tests of your life really do become your testimony of how God patched you up, and those scars become the transformed golden pathway into the beautiful you that you have become, and your true God-given destiny will open right before your eyes. There is so much more that God has waiting for you whether you are 2, 22, 52, or 92.

Once you take those first fledging steps of faith, each successive one becomes easier. The path may still be winding and may still seem uphill for a while, but you've got a navigator that knows where every pothole, crack, and bump in the road is located, and He will steer you clear of them if you just listen to your spiritual GPS, the Holy Spirit. He knows how the enemy will try and trip you up, so He wrote a whole book of instructions mapping them out. The Holy Bible is your life atlas. It's mapped out everything you need to make it through this life safely and get to your final destination in heaven. Your life trip was never designed to be only challenges, even though it can feel that way sometimes. God designed and equipped you perfectly for your journey. He has placed signposts and warnings along the way, as well as adventures and fun. Try not to miss either of them. Life is too short not to walk in the fullness of what God planned for you.

You may not realize that God has offered a covenant to you. Yes—you! The New and Everlasting Covenant of eternal life is offered to every single person on earth. "For God so loved the world that He gave His one and only Son, that whoever believes in Him shall not perish but have eternal life" (John 3:16 NIV). If you still haven't found the faith to believe this scripture, I encourage you to ask God to give you an encounter with His son, Jesus Christ, that you might see and believe in the One who came to save your life and receive Him as your Lord and Savior. You really only need a mustard seed of faith to see miracles manifest into your life. When you choose Christ, everything changes both now and forever. And trust me, forever is a really long time. You will not

When you choose Christ, everything changes both now and forever

only change history, but you will become an eternity changer in the process as well. Now you have to admit that is pretty amazing, right?

Besides, becoming an heir to the kingdom of God has some pretty phenomenal perks, or did you forget about the dunamis power of the Holy Spirit? Speaking in tongues, healing every imaginable affliction, kicking demons to the curb, raising up dead people, as well as influencing everyone in your life just by mentioning Jesus' name. Hey, miracles, signs, and wonders are fun; you definitely need to try this supernatural life in Jesus. There's a whole world of people just waiting for you to be their one. The one who changes everything they ever thought about God. The one who instills hope into their hopeless lives. The one who restores sight, hearing, and the will to live through the miracle-working name of Jesus Christ. You may be their only one, and they may be your only one. You genuinely don't want to miss the opportunity to introduce your world to the One who saved your life, Jesus Christ.

There's a beautiful Bible verse that says, "The LORD your God is in your midst, a Warrior who saves. He will rejoice over you with joy; He will be quiet in His love [making no mention of your past sins], He will rejoice over you with shouts of joy" (Zephaniah 3:17, AMP). I wish someone would have told me this verse a really long time ago; that God was with me and rejoiced over me with joy. Because then I could have stood on the Bible verse that says, "for the joy of the LORD is your strength" (Nehemiah 8:10 NIV). If your life has been anything like mine, you could have used some joy in it a lot sooner, and getting some strength from the Lord would have been immensely helpful too. So I say that over you now, that God is rejoicing over you, and His joy will be your strength. Because God cares for you no matter what your circumstances may look like now, and He is working all things for your good no matter how long it may take to happen. Now you can share that word with someone else who really needs to hear it too.

Every day, we are in the process of transforming our minds and conforming them to what Christ has to say about us. He says we are forgiven, we are chosen, we are loved, we are His children, we are seated in heavenly places, and we are heirs to the kingdom of God. I think Paul summed up what the kingdom of God is when he wrote, "For the kingdom of God is not a matter of eating and drinking but of righteousness and peace and joy in the Holy Spirit" (Romans 14:17 NIV). So when we choose Christ, we inherit His righteousness; peace is when we walk in harmony with the Prince of Peace, and joy is the most personal choice of all. It isn't earned or given or won; rather, it's a state of being that we attain as our minds are transformed by believing and living into every word that proceeds from the mouth of God.[3]

God is truth, and God is love above all other things.[4] Jesus and the Holy Spirit combine with the Father to comprise the Triune Godhead to complete all truth and all love that exists. You are included in that picture when you believe in what Jesus did for you and accept Him as your Lord and Savior and receive the infilling of the Holy Spirit. The Holy Spirit is the Spirit of Jesus Christ living in you here and now. Jesus abiding in me is what I experienced in Brazil in an extraordinary manifestation of the Holy Spirit. That is what I wish for every person on earth. "So that Christ may dwell in your hearts through faith; and that you, being rooted and grounded in love, may be able to comprehend with all the saints what is the breadth and length and height and depth, and to know the love of Christ which surpasses knowledge, that you may be filled up to all the fullness of God" (Ephesians 3:17-19 ESV).

I pray that each and every one of you be filled with the continuous, unending, unsurpassed love and joy of Christ and that it floods your spirit, causing an unquenchable hope to rise up from deep within your heart and very soul. I pray that parts of your being that have never known true love are awakened

---

[3] "But He answered and said, 'It is written, 'Man shall not live by bread alone, but by every word that proceeds from the mouth of God.'" Matthew 4:4 NKJV

[4] "Three things will last forever—faith, hope, and love—and the greatest of these is love." 1 Corinthians 13:13 NLT.

and enlightened in a marvelous swirl of deep emotion. That Jesus touches the very essence of who you are and who you were created to be. That your spirit knows your Creator and recognizes an unfathomable love that your mind can scarcely comprehend. That your spirit experiences the fullness of perfect love, perfect joy, perfect peace, perfect everything. That in those first moments of bliss, the entirety of who you are transcends the physical world and all that you have ever known was possible.

That you experience a tenderness and understanding that permeates right into your bones. That a desire rises up in you to know and be known and that you feel an utter unconditional acceptance of who you are. That Jesus' gentleness soothes every anxiety or concern you may have. That you know the goodness and purity of His intent and feel the total contentment of space and time. That you are wrapped in a sense of complete trust and safety as if the whole world just came to a stop and was held in perfect stillness. That you will be captivated and totally apprehended by a love that reaches in and touches every part of you and every part of everything that ever was or will be.

I pray that you will now know there is a love so much greater than anything that exists in the physical world. That there exists a love that no human words can adequately describe or portray. That there is a loving God, and His love outweighs every problem, every disappointment, and every crushing pain that you have ever borne. That there is a God of unimaginable love and of such magnitude of power that nothing in this world could possibly match or equal. That there is a God of such complexity and completeness that this world cannot contain or explain Him. That there is a God that superseded everything known to man. That there is a God of such utter magnificence that all thoughts of this world cease to matter. Nothing in all the world can compare, and His name is Jesus Christ.

I pray that you encounter Jesus in such a powerful way and that you let Him shatter your disbelief, your fear, your past, and everything that has held you back from the truth that Jesus whispered into my heart that very first morning: "'For I know the plans I have for you,' declares the LORD, 'plans to prosper you and not to harm you, plans to give you hope and a future'" (Jeremiah 29:11 NIV). May the hope of the world, Jesus Christ, permeate every part of who you are and bring you into the fullness of the beautiful future He has for you. Amen.

There is a God of such complexity and completeness that this world cannot contain or explain Him. That God is loving, and His love outweighs every problem, every disappointment, and every crushing pain you have ever borne.

Appendix

Recommended Reading List

- Lundy Bancroft, *Why Does He do That?* (New York, NY: The Berkeley Publishing Group, 2002).

- Randy Clark, *There is More, The Secret to Experiencing God's Power to Change Your Life* (Bloomington MN: Chosen Books, Baker Publishing Group, 2013).

- Henry Cloud, John Townsend, *Boundaries* (Grand Rapids, MI: Harper Collins Publishers, 1992, 2017).

- Kimberly Daniels, *Give It Back! God's Weapons for Turning Evil to Good* (Lake Mary, FL: Charisma House, 2007).

- John Fergusson, *Authority* (Auckland, New Zealand: JF Ministries, 2010).

- Kenneth Hagin, *Believer's Authority* (Tulsa, OK: Faith Library Publications, 1967, 1986).

- Leif Hetland, *Called to Reign, Living and Loving From a Place of Rest* (New York, NY: Convergence Press, 2017).

- Mike Hutchings, *Supernatural Freedom from the Captivity of Trauma: Overcoming the Hindrance to Your Wholeness* (Shippensburg, PA: Destiny Image Publishers, Inc., 2021).

- David Jeremiah, *Overcomer* (Nashville, TN: W Publishing, 2018).

- Bill Johnson, *The Supernatural Power of a Transformed Mind* (Shippensburg, PA: Destiny Image Publishers, Inc., 2014).

- Caroline Leaf, *Switch On Your Brain, The Key to Peak Happiness, Thinking and Health* (Grand Rapids, MI: Baker Books a division of Baker Publishing Group, 2013).

- Neal Lozano, *Unbound* (Grand Rapids, MI: Chosen Books, 2003, 2010).

- Derek Prince, *They Shall Expel Demons* (Grand Rapids, MI: Chosen Books, 1998).

- Joseph Prince, *Destined to Reign* (Tulsa, Ok: Harrison House Publishers, 2007).

- Benjamin Williams and Micah Joy Williams, *The Basics in 21 Days* (Benjamin Williams and Micah Joy Williams, 2011).

About the Author

Suzanne Kutz

Suzanne Kutz has twenty years of experience in executive administration within higher education, including strengths in strategic planning, leadership, and management. However, all of that was superseded in the summer of 2010 when God spoke audibly to Suzanne, which changed the entire trajectory of her life. That extraordinary encounter with Jesus changed everything she ever knew about her Christian faith and caused her to re-examine her entire belief system. The resultant zeal and love of Christ has catapulted her into a miracle-filled life devoted to sharing the Good News of Jesus Christ with the world.

Sue has a gift for instilling Kingdom mindsets in all walks of life and spheres of influence and has been especially blessed with the Holy Spirit's gifts of prophecy and healing. Sue is committed to assisting the body of Christ around the world in spiritual training and education, inner healing, deliverance, spiritual mentoring, and inspirational speaking. The proud mother of two beautiful daughters and one incredible grandchild, Sue is an avid reader and lover of all things in nature. She was born and raised in Pennsylvania but now calls Dallas, Texas her home.

To learn more or to invite
Sue to minister:

suzanne-kutz.com